The Cardinal in the Snow

Where do I go from here?

John A. Kenney

Parson's Porch Books

The *Cardinal* in the Snow
ISBN: Softcover
Copyright © 2023 by John A. Kenney

Parson's Porch Books is an imprint of Parson's Porch & Company (PP&C) in Cleveland, Tennessee. PP&C is a self-funded charity which earns money by publishing books of noted authors, representing all genres. Its face and voice is **David Russell Tullock** (dtullock@parsonsporch.com).

Parson's Porch & Company *turns books into bread & milk* by sharing its profits with the poor.

www.parsonsporch.com

The Cardinal in the Snow

Dedication

Jane and I have been married for over 51 years. Jane has listened to and made invaluable suggestions for nearly all my jury arguments before they have been delivered. She has done the same for many talks and speeches over the years. Now, as our focus has changed, she is still there—reading over, listening to and providing insightful thoughts, comments and suggestions for every sermon and every outline for talks to Church classes and groups. Her faith is strong, solid and everlasting. That comfortable underpinning in her faith has permeated many of my thoughts and have made their way into this book. She has read and made comments and suggestions for each of the many drafts of the pages in this book.

My life is made better every day with her.

Contents

Acknowledgments

Several people provided the encouragement and very helpful constructive review needed to complete this project. First, Rev. Dr. Paul Kirbas, PhD, and Rev. Glenn Dunn encouraged my attending the Austin Presbyterian Theological Seminary CIM program. The professors and classes there, when coupled with the additional research and reading stimulated by the classes, speakers and discussions, added needed theological backdrop for this work. I particularly appreciated the leadership of Rev. Dr. Ted Wardlaw, PhD, as seminary president, in fostering the stimulating environment I enjoyed. Dr Wardlaw's outstanding successor, Rev. Dr. José Irizarry, PhD, has provided encouragement and help in the publication process.

Rev. Dr. Cynthia Rigby, PhD, has been extraordinarily encouraging and helpful in her thoughtful and theologically stimulating discussions. She introduced me to the editor of this book, Caitlin Parsons. Caitlin has provided her invaluable editing experience along with thoughts, comments and tips for completion of the work.

Paige Bass, Mike Bass, Rev. Glenn Dunn, my brother-in-law John Francis, PhD, Rev. Paul Kirbas, PhD, Rev. Jennifer Kirbas, Randy McClanahan, Hon. David Russell, Dana Russell, Jim Sharrock, Nancy Sharrock and Rev. Landon Whitsett read drafts and provided many helpful comments and suggestions.

Introduction

Where do I go from here?

Beauty in God's world is everywhere. In fact, it is so all encompassing, it is too easy to run along through life and never really "see" what is all around. Oh sure, a great work of art, a sculpture, a little beaming child, a cuddly puppy, a field of flowers—I may notice those and pause a moment to take it in, but otherwise the pressures of schedule, personal interactions, work and just living in our complicated world can take over and block the "view."

One early winter morning, a string of record-breaking bitter cold days was overlain by several inches of un-melting snow. I rounded the corner into the back room of our warm home and saw it: A bright red cardinal sitting on a barren branch of a small tree just outside the window. It was all puffed up and fat looking, but I knew, from an article I read just the day before, that birds fluff up like that to keep as warm as possible in the bitter cold. In the frame of the window, it was a perfect picture in nature's brilliant red against a backdrop of white snow. At first, I only thought of what a neat photo this would make and hurried for my phone camera.

As I took several pictures, I realized—the cardinal was not enjoying the scenery and waiting patiently for me to get just the right picture. No, it was waiting for more seed to fill the empty bird feeder hanging in the little tree.

It was a beautiful, solitary, probably lonely and very hungry figure.

As I looked at the photos I took that morning—before I put on my coat, hat and boots and hurried out to fill the feeder with a new supply of seeds—I realized the contrasts of life were framed for me in that window. There I was, warm and comfortable inside my home. The awesome beauty of just one little bird so brilliantly adorned by God's plan for a world of beauty, love and fullness was ever present. But the scene was overshadowed by what I knew was a life-threatening circumstance for that creature. If the feeder was not replenished with food that provided it nourishment and the warmth of the energy it would create, the bird would likely perish.

Every one of God's human children are a creation of intense beauty and awesome value. How often are those having difficulties left out in the "cold" by those inside where it is "warm"? How many of us, through pride or fear or both, stay puffed up and are never willing to show or say what we really need even when times are tough and maybe even desperate?

Think about that bird if you are the one in need or if you are the one wondering if another needs help. *Do something*, whatever your situation, and the beauty of life will shine in the next picture painted by your God. That cardinal did. It came to the place it knew (had faith) food would be—and it waited—and was rewarded. I was rewarded as well. I saw the beauty and meaning of God's creation in a more striking way that day.

I generally think of myself as the person in the warm home. I am doing fine. My needs are met but I know there can be and is more for me out there in this sometimes cold, chaotic world. This does not mean there have not been times when I have felt the cold and storm clouds of that world. I expect most everyone has felt both the "warmth" and the "cold" from time to time. Both are a part of the fabric of life. There are similar, if not identical, actions that can smooth out the temperatures of life. Life on this earth does not have to be just a path to life in heaven with our God. Our earthly objectives change or can be refocused to the beauty, grandeur and joy of the world in which we live. Rough and cold spots will still occur. Questions and feelings that I do not understand will be there from time to time. But with our heart and mind focused on faith in our day-to-day lives, each of us can find that "heaven on earth" that is often mentioned but often so elusive.

Where do I go from here?

This book is my humble effort to share my long-developing thoughts, sharpened while studying seminary courses and crystalized after that cold early winter morning. Hopefully, as you read and consider and discuss the thoughts, suggestions and questions spaced throughout the book, you will find your answers to the questions:

Where do I go from here?
How do I find the "heaven on earth" that God has in store for me?

As a further preface, I will admit I have always been a bit of a science nerd. For example, I really enjoyed the challenge of math in high school. But then, I did not really understand its purpose beyond being able to add the money I made working at the grocery store and subtracting the cost of the 1958 Chevy I bought with it. I, of course, wanted a 1957 Chevy. It, in my opinion at the time—and today for that matter—was infinitely "cooler" looking. But, my addition and subtraction told me I did not and would not have enough money to buy that in the foreseeable future.

My appreciation for math matured quickly when I decided to study engineering at the University of Oklahoma. I soon understood that math was one of the fundamental tools that allows us to design and build those cars and so many other things.

I also learned what is generally known as the scientific or engineering method. In a methodical and step-by-step application, it involves:

(1) Identification of a problem,
(2) assembling relevant facts,
(3) analyzing those facts using applicable mathematical and other tools,
(4) developing alternatives,
(5) testing or trying those alternatives and,
(6) through this trial and error, eventually arriving at a solution to a problem.

It was not until years after engineering school and law school, and after attending the school of "hard knocks" for far too long, that I came to realize that the basic steps of the engineering/scientific method can be applied to help solve or mitigate many problems in life. The steps that can work in helping one to solve life's inevitable problems may have different labels but have the same function. They help us get our hands, head and heart around figuring out what to do next. As we proceed, you will see an outline of how all of us can apply these steps to guide, and hopefully solidify, our thoughts and plans for the future of our life adventure.

I believe life is or can be an adventure, an awesome adventure. Many writers and speakers refer to life as a "journey." But the term "journey" implies, to me, something different. I attribute a journey to a trip with a degree of difficulty and sometimes exhausting toil involved. Life does not have to be like that. There will be tough times but the overall mystery and excitement for what is next can overpower and permeate life. Yes, it becomes an adventure. All that is needed is faith and trust in God.

I make that sound easy and we all know it is not. But, read aloud and listen in your mind and heart to 1 Peter 1:18–25:

> [18] You know that you were ransomed from the futile ways inherited from your ancestors, not with perishable things like silver or gold, [19] but with the precious blood of Christ, like that of a lamb without defect or blemish. [20] He was destined before the foundation of the world,

but was revealed at the end of the ages for your sake. [21] Through him you have come to trust in God, who raised him from the dead and gave him glory, so that your faith and hope are set on God. [22] Now that you have purified your souls by your obedience to the truth so that you have genuine mutual love, love one another deeply from the heart. [23] You have been born anew, not of perishable but of imperishable seed, through the living and enduring word of God. [24] "For all flesh is like grass and all its glory like the flower of grass. The grass withers, and the flower falls, [25] but the word of the Lord endures forever."

Belief, faith, love of God and mutual love of our fellow persons will lead to a new birth and life of adventure that will endure forever—in that Heaven on Earth and beyond!

The sight of the cardinal in the snow leads to more thoughts. How do I help? Can I fill the feeder with seed? Is there more I can do to make a difference in a cold world? What can I do to generate warmth, not only for others, but for myself as well? Maybe I can fill with seeds *a feeder that I have built*! Yes, how do I find where I go from here? We all need renewal from time to time. Let's follow the lead of that cardinal in the snow who fostered the thoughts we will talk about here: have faith and act. As we will see, things will be different and better the next time we check our temperature.

I have recharacterized the steps of the engineering/scientific method as Cardinal Steps for solving life's problem and questions. These steps are applicable to finding your next phase in the life adventure. They also can be applied in solving problems that appear in everyday life. The issues that arise in everyday life appear on short notice. There is not usually time to methodically apply each Cardinal Step. But they can be made easier if one has addressed these steps with a "big picture" point of view. After we do that, we will see if we can find some useful everyday decision-making tips.

Cardinal Steps

Cardinal Step 1: Identify the problem
Cardinal Step 2: Assemble the facts
Cardinal Step 3: Analyze the facts (using tools of faith)
Cardinal Step 4: Develop alternatives
Cardinal Step 5: Test or try out alternatives
Cardinal Step 6: Go for it!

We will work our way through each step and see where we end up.

Notes

Chapter One:

To set the stage—my own experience

This book is partially the result of my own search for the next step in a life that has generally been very fulfilling. I first worked as an engineer and then obtained a law degree. As a lawyer I continued work in areas involving engineering, science and technology for my entire career. One day, not long enough ago, I looked up while I was considering taking on a new law case. That would probably mean two or three more years of doing the same thing I had always done. I suddenly paused and realized it was time to retire (or, sort of retire, and stop trying cases, at least). And—a surprise to myself and, I know, my wife—I actually did it. But then, what was next?

I had always been on the go and "involved" and was not ready to give up either of those things. I had developed several interests/hobbies over the years and assumed those would occupy my time. I gave each of them some study. I have written lyrics and produced some country western songs and CDs over the last few years. But, I realized, though the lyrics were challenging and fun to develop, music is critical to a good song, no matter how engaging the lyrics. Being realistic, a musician I am not!

During my work with technology as an engineer and lawyer, I have been the inventor on some patents. I thought about developing a lab to do more of this work looking for new and innovative ideas. Soon, I focused on the reality of invention. I keep on my desk a framed quote of Albert Einstein. When questioned about discovery and how it occurs, he said:

"Discovery is not the result of logical thought, even though the end result is intimately bound to the rules of logic."

Something similar has been my experience in a much more mundane set of inventive experiences. For me, the thoughts that led to my patents just appeared in my mind without particular triggers, special investigation or "logical thought." In fact, when I have focused on a specific problem and sought to "invent" a solution, I have never been successful in finding something patentable. It sometimes ends up being a convoluted mess that is not always practical, let alone a novel solution. So, that work will have to await the serendipity of a new thought "appearing" on some unexpected day.

Other "future" ideas met similar ends.

Luckily, on one of those unexpected days, I had a conversation with my minister (at the time), Dr. Paul Kirbas. He had just become the President of the Graduate Theological Foundation, which provides graduate-level theology education worldwide. Earlier, with his encouragement and that of another friend and minister, Rev. Glenn Dunn, I had enrolled in the

Certificate in Ministry program at Austin Presbyterian Theological Seminary which I subsequently completed. Dr. Kirbas was scheduled to go to Oxford in England for a meeting and lecture series sponsored by the Foundation. During the conversation, he asked if I would like to go along.

I jumped at the opportunity and travelled with him to Oxford and participated in the events and meetings. It was fascinating and, in fact, comforting to meet with theologians from the Christian, Muslim and Jewish faiths from around the world. I came away with a confirmation of my long-held belief that all people are very much alike. Though we practice different religions, have different cultural backgrounds and speak different languages, we have very similar wants and desires for our future and the future of our children and families. There is hope that peace can come to all our lives. I believe that we can live side by side if we just focus on these common goals and not our differences.

I will take a short moment to relate an example. In many court cases, today, the people involved are required by the Court to participate in a mediation session with an independent mediator. There are some mediators that are more successful than others in helping litigants reach a settlement. These mediators focus the time in the session not on the differences of the parties but on finding the real goals and objectives of each that can be realistically fulfilled by a settlement. These can be different for each party and are usually different in every case. This can be as simple as identifying the desire of the parties to get the case over with and stop the expense. It can be as complicated as identifying and focusing on a business or financial solution where each meet some personal but different objective.

I recall the approach of one very skilled mediator. It sometimes happens that one party is not going to accept a clearly mutually beneficial solution on a complicated matter solely because of the desire to "win." The mediator would pull out a dollar bill from his own pocket and give it to one party to give to the reluctant party. A "win" was sometimes as simple as that for one party and as insignificant as that for the other. The case was usually settled.

I suspect the same phenomenon is involved in many of our world problems that lead to the devastation of war and hardship for many on both sides. If only our politicians and world leaders were required to go before a good independent mediator!

Now, back to my story. I think that trip and experience was a part of God's answer to my long-prayed "ask" for guidance on the future for my wife and me. The future became clearer almost overnight. I realized each of us really does have a role in our future. Every little bit we do collectively and synergistically can make a difference that can truly change the world. I hope to do my part, and it starts with this sharing of my thoughts here. Hopefully, others will be encouraged to share, care and do things that collectively make a difference, not only in their day-to-day lives, but in the lives of many others.

This book includes pages for notes so your thoughts can be jotted down as you read. Of course, many of you will make notes electronically while reading *and thinking*.

We will create notes and lists as we read that we will use to put together our thoughts and ideas for the future—our Cardinal Plan. These notes will likely change, be modified or be supplemented as we proceed. Remember—there is no right or wrong answer. Each of us will incorporate our own unique personal thoughts. But, discuss your thoughts with others if you are comfortable. There is always a benefit in listening to other ideas. Some may be helpful in constructing your Cardinal Plan.

We will also prepare our own Cardinal Rules to guide our future. These are thoughts and principles we will try to incorporate in our everyday life. Pages at the end of each section and at the end of the book are provided as a place to write down lists of alternatives for your future, for notes while developing your Cardinal Plan and identifying your personal Cardinal Rules. This book can then become a guide for thinking about the future. Or, it might become an index for even more notes on separate paper or in an electronic format for storage and updating.

Discussion:

1. Express your thoughts on how we can work with others even if we have differences.
2. What are your hopes and goals for your future?
3. Write down your thoughts and ideas of what you could do with others that you would enjoy and that could be of help to others in some way.

You will look back at these thoughts as we proceed.

Notes

Chapter Two

Cardinal Step 1: Identify the problem

Now, let's follow the Cardinal Steps to finding a life of faith, service and fulfillment. In the end, these steps can mature into your own Cardinal Plan and Cardinal Rules.

Most of us, at least from time to time, reach a point where things are going okay, but we just know there must be more to experience and accomplish in life on this earth. I have talked to people of all ages that have experienced the initial exhilaration of reaching a life milestone or event. Then, after a time, a feeling that there is or must be more appears. Some have described it as a searching or longing for a further life direction. These thoughts and questions can be summed up by asking: *Where do I go from here?*

That cardinal was sitting where it knew food was most likely to be available. Its beauty was shining on the backdrop of the new-fallen snow. It was waiting. Maybe that is each of us at times. The beauty of a life going well surrounds us but we are waiting for more. For many of us, our needs for the daily food we eat and drink are met. We have been given much. We then ask: What more is in store for me? Where do I go from here? Jesus summed it up in the last sentence of Luke 12:48:

> [48] … From everyone to whom much has been given, much will be required; and from the one to whom much has been entrusted, even more will be demanded.

Yes, God is never finished with us. There is always "more" for each of us to do. What a comfort; we will not be lost and wandering—God has more in store. Relax, do not worry. Jesus promised in Luke 48:29–31:

> [29] And do not keep striving for what you are to eat and what you are to drink, and do not keep worrying. [30] For it is the nations of the world that strive after all these things, and your Father knows that you need them. [31] Instead, strive for his kingdom, and these things will be given to you as well.

Mathew 6:33 confirms:

> [33] But strive first for the kingdom of God and his righteousness, and all these things will be given to you as well.

Everyone worries about things. Our need for fulfillment can be elusive. God knows this and knows what we are worrying about. Most importantly, God knows what we *need*. I have had to learn that what I think I need and what God knows I need are not always the same! Nevertheless, Jesus assures that our basic needs will be met, and the door is open for many more good things for each of us. Moreover, God will grant to each of us a glimpse of "heaven on earth" or, at least, a "heaven on earth" feeling if we work in God's light and do our best to live as God would have us live while here on earth.

C. S. Lewis summed it up when he concluded: "Joy is the serious business of Heaven." True joy can and does happen right here on earth. Heaven may not be here but a glimpse of it may be. Think about the feeling of awe and wonder when you see a newborn baby. What about the beauty of a field of sunflowers blooming and glistening in the noonday sun, or some yellow daffodils in a vase on a windowsill? There can be an amazing feeling of warmth and comfort from the hug of a loved one or from a tight squeeze and little squeal of a child in a moment of greeting. That joy may be momentary, but the feeling of love from and of God and of God's creations in those moments—*that* is what I am talking about.

I remember, many years ago, as I sat on a hill in front of a little abandoned chapel and watched the farmers walking home from a long day's work, time seemed to stand still. The beauty of God's creation streamed over me, carried by the rays of the setting sun. I actually thought for a moment I could feel the prayers of others echoing from the walls behind me.

It was one late afternoon in the heart of Mexico near San Miguel de Allende. Young vacationing couples (like my wife and me and our friends) in those days could easily drive to San Miguel from Houston. So, we did. There was a natural spring outside of San

Miguel where a large spring-fed swimming pool had been constructed and we went there for a lazy summer afternoon. After swimming for a while, the others wanted to sit in the sun. But I decided to climb the hill behind us up to the bluff and see what was in that little building I saw in the distance.

The climb opened up before me as beautiful a view as I will ever experience. The sun was low in the west and the distant sound of church bells began calling the farmers home for the day. After sitting for a while, I stood and walked inside the little building. It was made of adobe and was clearly a chapel with an adobe altar still in place. There was not much else inside, and it looked as if it had been abandoned many years ago. I went back to my seat on the stone and wondered why it was abandoned. I never learned the answer to that question. But, I did feel a sense of peace and comfort, like I am sure many others did before me, knowing that only God could create such an opportunity of serenity and beauty. That joy of the moment, perhaps a feeling of a little bit of heaven, can and does happen to us all. C. S. Lewis focuses on this in his book *Mere Christianity*. God is with us on earth and dwells within us in the Holy Spirit. Jesus, in the Sermon on the Mount, gave us the Lord's Prayer which includes: "Thy will be done on earth as it is in heaven." In *Mere Christianity*, Lewis pointedly places this in perspective: "Aim at Heaven and you will get earth 'thrown in': aim at earth and you will get neither."

It may sound unrealistic to say "Aim at Heaven." It is not. I bet you can think of moments and times where amazingly wonderful or happy and unexpected things happened. Thank God when they happen for you. Savor them and that same feeling of joy, those moments of faith manifested right here on earth, can grow and surround you.

Part of our effort here is to find and focus on the opportunity for those moments to manifest in my life more and more often?

Let's get started. Cardinal Step 1 is to "identify the problem." It may be as simple as seeking the answer to: "Where do I go from here?" That was the "problem" I identified as I thought about retiring from my law practice. Others may identify things more specific such as: "I am lonely"; "Should I take a new job or project?"; "I am just not happy"; "Is there something more?"; or other individually specific things.

Answering some questions might help with this first Cardinal Step. (Remember, we are identifying the problem. We will work on finding answers or solutions as we proceed.)

First, consider your recurring "feelings." Be open with yourself about these "feelings" and your answers to these questions and record your answers:

A. Do you feel content in your life? Is this your feeling most days, some days or not many days?
B. When you feel frustrated, what are the sources of this feeling?
C. Do you have the "I never do anything" feeling?

D. Do you feel you are just doing the same things over and over?

E. Do you feel bored even though you are busy?

F. How do you feel when things go wrong?

G. What makes you angry? Who and what are the sources of this feeling?

H. Has a loved one or close friend passed away? Have you lost a relationship with another person?

I. Have you been disappointed that something has not gone as you expected or hoped?

J. Are there other recurring "feelings" that you would like to address?

Next, answer these questions:

A. If you answered that you feel content most or some of the time, what are you doing when you feel content?

B. What makes you happy? How often do you feel happy? What are you doing at those times?

C. What would you like to do that might make you feel content and happy more often?

D. How do you feel after a success? Are you satisfied to enjoy it? Do you look for the next challenge?

Now, consider these questions:

A. Do you get angry reading things in print, on the internet or listening to TV?

B. How much time do you spend a day on the internet and/or listening to TV?

C. Can you reduce this electronic media time?

D. What interactions do you have with others daily that are not required by work?

E. How often do you have Interactions with new people?

One short comment—I remember a time a friend seemed upset nearly all the time about something that appeared in the news or media. Some of the media keeps our attention by presenting things that play on our emotions both good and bad. When my friend realized this and reduced the time each day occupied by electronic media, they focused on other things that included more interactions with other people, which produced more days of contentment and happiness. If this is applicable to you, it could be helpful to work on this so that the—sometimes powerful—overlay will be reduced. Thoughts will be opened to other things and more time will be available for personal interactions.

F. What motivates you to get involved in something?

G. Where are you in your life? Are you doing okay but feel like and hope there is more for you to learn and do?

H. Do you know others that have expressed the same or similar feelings? If you are comfortable, discuss your answers to these questions with others.

Review your answers. Do they group into categories? Which of the things you have identified are things you can realistically work on solving or changing? Which would you like to perpetuate and expand? What did you identify that motivates you to action on a problem?

Write down any conclusions. You may use these conclusions as a guide in your further efforts from here to the end of this Cardinal Exercise.

As an example, I did this exercise myself. I had a successful law practice. I was content. Nevertheless, I had a nagging feeling I could do more for others that would use my gifts and talents, as limited as they may be. I also felt I had more to learn in my faith. I wondered where learning more about it would lead. I thought: "Where do I go from here?" That was the problem I sought to solve.

One important point: Remember that significant depression, "dark" feelings, anger or other intense negative emotions may have bubbled out in your thoughts while answering the questions. Be honest with yourself. The care and guidance of a professional may be important.

Hopefully, this exercise has been successful. Identify and write down the "problem" or "problems" you would like to solve. Do not worry if you are not sure of your identification or description. This is a start and there is plenty more to go that may help you narrow or better identify your objectives.

Notes

Chapter Three

Cardinal Step 2: Assemble the facts

Let's now search for an answer or solution to the "problems" identified.

What are the facts applicable to my problem-solving and discovery journey? The facts will be unique for each of us, just as we are each unique. Relevant facts will vary from person to person. They will be somewhere between "somewhat" and "dramatically" different. No matter what, they will not likely be exactly the same. Spend some time thinking about what applies to you. There are some generalities that may help guide this effort; as you work through this process, make notes of your thoughts resulting from each exercise.

First, ask yourself again the question: Where am I in my life? This is not necessarily an age question. Many of us reach points at different ages where we realize we are okay but may feel lonely, a bit lost or feel just as if marking time.

Are you "waiting" for something to happen—like that cardinal? It was all fluffed up and probably was warm enough. It knew food would show up and was in the place where it appeared every day. Otherwise, it was sitting on the branch and just waiting.

Are you are doing something that accomplishes the satisfaction of the daily needs of your life yet have a feeling, maybe one gnawing at your inner spirit, there could be a more meaningful life there if you just knew how to find it?

These feelings and this questioning can appear after reaching a life milestone. These include graduation, job or vocation-related events, a long-sought success and/or recognition by others for some accomplishment. Milestones may also occur during or after family events, births, marriage, partnerships, retirement and at many other life events. Moreover, we all know things do not always go as planned or hoped. This can include personal breakups and losses, job or vocation-related events like lack of promotion or job loss, home changes including life changing events such as leaving home, loved ones leaving home or town, friendships that are changed or lost, the passing of loved ones and on and on.

Of course, often these "stages" or "times" of life seem to be driven by age. Becoming age 21, 30 or 40, the empty nest syndrome that occurs for many in their forties or early fifties, the middle age "crazies" some associate with age 50, retirement in one's sixties or seventies, etc. are all examples that may or may not apply to any one of us.

Think about this: There is always time for more. Never assume anything is over or it is too late to do something. Most of Albert Einstein's amazing discoveries occurred when he was in his twenties, yet he impacted the world in his writings and actions the rest of his life. Colonel Sanders did not start his namesake franchised chicken restaurants until he was in his sixties. Wally Funk, a woman who had a lifelong career as a pilot, flight instructor and air safety investigator pilot, was part of an early NASA program for female astronauts but never got to fly in space. Not until she was 82, at least! In 2021, she became the oldest person to fly in space on Blue Origin's first civilian space flight. How about astronaut and U.S. Senator John Glenn? In 1998, he became the oldest person to travel to space at age 77 on the space shuttle Discovery. There, he participated in health studies related to problems associated with aging. President George H. W. Bush made a sky dive at age 90. I expect at some time in each of their lives, these events seemed out of reach or a dream and not a likelihood.

Can you identify other similar events in the life of people you know? What about in your life? Are there things that seemed out of reach that suddenly were there for the experiencing and doing? What facts are applicable to you and your life right now? Write them down.

Reality is a common thread in the search for an answer to the question: Where do I go from here? A focus on why one feels this way and relating that feeling to current circumstances can help in finding the answer. For example, things that can be done when a person is retired may not reasonably be available to one who is not able to retire. The responsibilities of home, family or children may restrict the options at one or more times in life. Those in their twenties may need to focus on getting a good foundation in place for a future and find it harder to focus on much else. Awareness of "your" facts can make a huge difference not only for you but for others that we can help.

Health is another factor in determining what is realistic. Restrictions that health imposes can modify or change options. Those restrictions can also be directional. By that I mean, there is always something one can do, and considering health issues can provide unique directions for focus. A person with heath limitations can talk by phone or electronic media with another in the same situation. An extraordinary example is the physicist Stephen Hawking. He became paralyzed with amyotrophic lateral sclerosis (ALS) and gradually, due to complications, became unable to speak from 1985 until his death in 2018. He communicated by electronic means, ultimately controlling the device by using only a face muscle. Nevertheless, before his death he continued his research, travelled the word lecturing and wrote several books including the best seller *A Brief History of Time* and related books that followed. Hawking's accomplishments are beyond extraordinary. The point is: There is always more one can do!

Sharing ideas and information about common issues and thoughts can be an amazing help. There are always others that can benefit from the actions of another. For example, the actions of one can have an important and very meaningful impact if only directed to others similarly situated. An overly busy working student can meet with another to do school homework. A busy mother or father juggling work and family responsibilities can give support to another by phone, social media or visits while waiting to pick up or deliver children somewhere. One can call a friend on a walk or drive home, volunteer on a Saturday morning at a food pantry, and many other fulfilling things if one focuses on "doing."

Are there restrictions you must incorporate in your looking to the future? Do they really have to be a restriction? If so, how can you incorporate this in your future life goals and plans? Write your thoughts down.

Identification of the spiritual, physical, mental and other gifts one has can be crucial to this exercise. Some are good speakers, some good thinkers and planners, some get things done, some have notoriety, some like the quiet, simple things, some like constant activity, some are introverted, some are extroverts, and on and on. But, no matter what our gifts, we each have them.

Anyone can identify personal abilities, experiences and/or traits as things others see as a "gift." It can be as simple as reading a book or article and sending it, or a note about it, to someone who would enjoy it. It can be as complicated as organizing a charity event that impacts thousands. Those broadly different actions both can positively impact another, and who is to say or know which is more important? If one can positively impact the life of another, that act is crucial to our world being a better place for all.

So, write down your gifts. Think about and offer God thanks for them every day.

Next, consider the things you like to do and enjoy. What are your favorite pastimes? Yes, this journey and life in general should be fun, so make it that kind of exercise! Ask yourself:

Who do you interact with on a regular basis?
What do you enjoy about that?
Where do you like to go and what happens there?
What are your interests, both outside the home and in?
What are your hobbies, now or in the past?

Answering questions like these can precede insight. You might discover things about yourself you never before realized. Write them down!

What are your goals and hopes or wishes for your future? Be honest with yourself and focus on what you really want, not what someone else wants or wants for you. After all, only you are going to see what you write down unless you choose to share it. Does this change your thoughts about what might and could be next for you? It just might! Write those down.

Next, allow yourself to dream. What do you see for you in your most wishful dreams? Remember, in this exercise, nothing is holding you back. Go for it. Write down those crazy ideas. One never knows where these might lead if they are tempered only a bit by reality.

And, just as important, is there something else? One of the questions I learned to ask at the end of interviewing a possible witness for a trial is: "Is there anything else I should have asked, or is there anything else I should know that I did not ask about or give you the opportunity to tell me?" It has been amazing how many times that question has uncovered previously unknown, very important and sometimes case-changing information. Answering that question might uncover life-changing information for you.

Finally, what have you been wondering since you started this exercise? Are you asking why is "this" not mentioned here? There will be something, I suspect. Be sure to think through that and write down anything else you identify that should be on your list of facts, thoughts, cares, concerns or important facts.

Now, look these notes over tomorrow. These "facts," when combined, can coalesce into something remarkable. A direction that never before was a part of your future. Renewing this process periodically, even after you have completed this Cardinal Exercise, can lead to even more new ideas, thoughts and opportunities.

With the facts documented, let's move on.

Discussion:

1. Take your notes on each of the questions above and sort through them for the key thoughts. Summarize those.
2. Try to condense the results of those notes into a paragraph. Share it with others if, and only if, you are comfortable.
3. Next, condense your paragraph and your notes of discussions with others into a single paragraph.
4. Finally, see if you can further condense this into a sentence. (Do not worry if you cannot do this, but trying can be helpful to get even better focus on the basic facts.) What ideas and thoughts made their way to that one sentence or came further into focus? Memorize the result. Maybe that is a place to start when you begin working on your Cardinal Plan.

Notes

Chapter Four

Cardinal Step 3: Analyze the facts (using tools of faith)

Our cardinal was sitting where it knew food had appeared the last few days. Our human processes are much different in sophistication. Logic is real and our brain power allows true analysis of our situations and the world. Nevertheless, we are also creatures of habit at times. We can be stuck and unable to see our way beyond the present. The tools we have available through our faith can overcome this malaise and will guide us to the food of true life. Let's discuss those tools and their application.

Tool 1: Read the Bible

2 Timothy 3:16–17:

[16] All scripture is inspired by God and is useful for teaching, for reproof, for correction, and for training in righteousness, [17] so that everyone who belongs to God may be proficient, equipped <u>for every good work</u>.

In my mind, the most obvious tool is the written Word—the Bible. 2 Timothy 3:16–17 is clear: Scripture readies one for "every good work." It is the place to start. One can be ready for the good life ahead and will be "equipped" to find that good life that is open to each of us by reading and using the Bible as a guide Today, our capabilities to gather information in the process of making up our own mind have taken a dramatic leap forward. Everyday access to the internet brings a new array of research tools. It is fascinating that what may be key information can now be pulled out of obscurity on a shelf in a remote library and is nearly instantly available to nearly anywhere we are located.

Consider the limitations on individual research and reading of the Bible and biblical materials for the average person even seventy-five years ago. Libraries were available with indexes for theological research. These were, at best, available to faculty and students and others with access to those libraries and the materials on the shelves. Moreover, the content on those shelves was selected by persons with many different points of view, which could limit what was selected for inclusion.

The Dead Sea Scrolls are a good example. Most of the scrolls were discovered in the 1940s hidden in caves and other places in the cliffs of the desert along the Jordan river and the banks of the Dead Sea. Unfortunately, after discovery, some of the scrolls and fragments of scrolls were plundered and lost to public access. Nevertheless, many have been preserved and protected. A number of authors have detailed the discovery and meticulous process of authenticating, unrolling and photographing, which took years. Today, the text and electronically duplicated copies of most of the preserved scrolls and fragments are available online. A straightforward search engine query will find any number of websites with access.

A further point about research—there have been literally hundreds of translations of the Bible or parts of the Bible over the centuries. Today, BibleGateway and other translation tabulating web sites include (at least) fifty English translations, and there are more available elsewhere. There are differences in these translations, and I leave it to you to decide which to read. Translation differences based upon the time of translation, the source of the original text used and many other factors have led to questions, debates and controversy about varying interpretations. One tip I learned from a seminary professor is to identify at least three translations that you believe are by credible, diligent and faithful translators. Then, when studying and preparing to discuss or talk about a particular Biblical text, I nearly always feel more comfortable in making up my own mind about the message of a particular text if I have read more than one translation.

Another practice I follow is to read the verses both before and after a particular Bible passage to be sure I understand the context of the verse. It is easy for me to misconstrue a single verse or excerpted quote from the Bible if I do not consider the context in which it is presented. And, a few verses may not be enough. Reading the entire chapter or even the entire book of the Bible can be necessary for me to feel I have the proper context.

Another thought: Luke 1:1–4 describes the reasons and process for the writing of the book:

^{1} Since many have undertaken to set down an orderly account of the events that have been fulfilled among us, ^{2} just as they were handed on to us by those who from the beginning were eyewitnesses and servants of the word, ^{3} I too decided, after investigating everything carefully from the very first, to write an orderly account for you, most excellent Theophilus, ^{4} so that you may know the truth concerning the things about which you have been instructed.

Considering this and other documentation and verification, I know the Bible is well written and researched, documented in the manner of the time, and records events and information with enough consistency from many sources so miraculous that I have faith, that our faith in it is justified. I believe the contents are truly divinely inspired. I try not to get overly concerned when I see differences in translations. There is more than enough for me to allow my understanding to guide my actions with the comfort that I have done my best to understand. This is what God expects of me, and God does not expect me or us to fully understand until the final day. We can grow every day in our understanding. See 2 Peter 3:18:

^{18} But grow in the grace and knowledge of our Lord and Savior Jesus Christ. To him be the glory both now and to the day of eternity. Amen.

I hope I live my life so that my knowledge can grow a bit every day. Likewise, the Lord's thoughts will always be beyond our expected understanding. We should not worry that we do not fully understand God's ways and thoughts.

Isaiah 55:8–9 confirms this:

> [8] For my thoughts are not your thoughts, nor are your ways my ways, says the Lord. [9] For as the heavens are higher than the earth, so are my ways higher than your ways and my thoughts than your thoughts.

I readily express my views to those that will listen. Nevertheless, I try not to attempt to force my views on others that have a different perspective or interpretation. I also know that I must listen to those with different interpretations or views. My wife sends me a devotional from one of several sources when she sees something I might like (or need!). It is great some days to see that theologians and practical preachers I respect have a thought similar to mine. But it is often even more exciting to see that they have a different idea, understanding or perspective on a point. Similarly, my wife will sometimes have a totally different thought about the meaning of a verse or passage from the Bible. I learn and grow in my understanding on those days.

Finally, for nearly every question I have about life, there is help in the Bible. Using a search engine and including the word "Bible" when asking for information on a topic or question will bring up an amazing array of writings and citations to Bible verses and texts that can be helpful. As an example, I decided to see if the Bible could help me think through and identify what might be identified as spiritual gifts. I did a search entry: "Bible Spiritual Gifts." That identified any number of tabulations, definitions and discussions of God's gifts found in several places in the Bible including: 1 Corinthians 12, Ephesians 4, 1 Peter 4 and Romans 12. I then read the citations and made a list that helped me to think about each one as it might apply to me. The list included: Administration, Apostleship, Discernment, Evangelism, Exhortation, Faith, Giving, Hospitality, Knowledge, Leadership, Mercy, Service, Shepherding, Teaching and Wisdom. Search engines can be an amazingly helpful tool! I have one caution to share: I always try to read critically and look for the credibility and sincerity of the authors and those who post their work. Double-check citations with rigor. I do not know how many times I have found a citation when taken in context to have a very different meaning than the point for which it is cited.

So, read the Bible! It is the starting place—the first tool in the cardinal process of analyzing the facts. Look up what the Bible has to say about the thoughts, ideas and musings that you have assembled in the "identification of the facts" work you have done. Make notes of what you have found in the Bible and keep those for later reference. They will never cease to be of value to you!

Discussion:

1. How often do you read the Bible? Do you make it a regular practice?
2. Do you read the Bible when you are worried or are seeking an answer to a problem? How does this help you find the answer you are seeking? Describe examples.
3. In compiling your list(s) as a part of this Cardinal Exercise, identify what reading the Bible has added, changed or modified on your list.

Notes

Tool 2: Study

Study is almost always a necessary part of a good decision-making process. Fruitful study is more than just thinking about something. It should be a deliberate process. It is, more importantly, often the key to making "wise" decisions. The importance of making decisions "wise" ones is dramatically summed up in Ecclesiastes 10:12:

> [12] Words spoken by the wise bring them favor, but the lips of fools consume them.

Over the years my wife has been a great keeper of notes and "takeaways" from sermons, Bible study lessons, interesting speakers and written articles. I tend to just sit and listen or read. For a long time, I liked to think I had important points filed away in my "steel-trap mind." I long suspected, and now know, that is not a sure thing. Some thoughts and pieces of information, maybe most, do escape from the trap! So, I also try to take some notes and we compare them later. I save and keep in files copies or links to articles and publications I have found helpful.

Every so often, I look over all my old files. When thinking about something and wondering what the Bible or thinkers on a topic have to say, I nearly always benefit from this review. Then, when combined with my recent notes and merged with thoughts from my wife and others, ideas emerge that are surprisingly fresh.

Hopefully, every sermon and many a lesson, verbal discussion, debate or speech has a takeaway or two that make sense to you, positive or negative. Make a few notes. File them somewhere—in digital memory or, for those of us a bit stuck in past practices, in a paper file folder. Add publications and link notes to these files. Periodically look them over. Study them when you are searching for an answer.

A deliberate study process involves more than reading and memorizing quotes or a list of points on a topic. I would like to think all the good ideas and insights come from me, but I know better. Study, as I have emphasized, necessarily includes reading, listening and considering the thoughts of others.

Years ago, I served as a court-appointed temporary judge on a court of appeals. Briefs were submitted by the parties and then two other temporary judges and I met as a panel on one or more occasions and discussed the case, the facts, the law and the result. I had my thoughts collected in each instance when we entered deliberations. However, several times, when we completed deliberations, some part of my thoughts changed or were modified by the good thoughts and perspectives of the other members of the panel. Other times, I left comfortable and confirmed that my thoughts were correct and right in the eyes of the law and justice. In each instance, I felt the exchange of ideas and points of view were critical to assuring that a right and just decision was sought and hopefully reached.

Similarly, the thoughts of others about life decisions and issues can make a difference in our thinking. Never be afraid to ask others for their thoughts. Such discussions can solidify our own ideas, change them completely or modify them for the better.

Caution is necessary, though. Not long ago, my wife and I were driving on a several-hour trip starting on Sunday morning. We decided to listen on the car radio to a vocally engaging radio and TV minister. The sermon and delivery were engaging, and we listened to three sermons during that drive. I enjoy listening to orators and learning what I can from their style and sometimes may not pay much attention to the message. That was the case for a while, but then I was caught up in the substance of the messages. All were different on their face but incorporated the same theme—faith in God can result in monetary prosperity. In my mind that is, in a way, possible. It is my observation that people that live a life that is based upon faith and doing their best to do the right thing will often find success, monetarily or just in the joy of living. A "prosperity gospel message," well delivered with stories of lottery winnings and financial windfalls, can be motivating, heartfelt and successful in bringing some to Christ. But when I think it over, there is a caution. Does God always solve our problems or bring financial success? Not always. Lack of success and failure does not mean that God has abandoned me. The chances of good and bad luck do not disappear. God lets us learn from mistakes, from tough times through events of our own making and from the chance of everyday life.

But, God is always with us and will get us through the tough times and bring us the joy of life in Christ. That is the true prosperity! These verses sum it up:

John 16:33:

> [33] I have said this to you, so that in me you may have peace. <u>In the world you face persecution. But take courage; I have conquered the world!</u>

Psalm 37:23–24:

> [23] Our steps are made firm by the LORD, when he delights in our way; [24] <u>though we stumble, we shall not fall headlong, for the LORD holds us by the hand.</u>

So, look beyond the façade—beyond the dramatic engaging speech, text or presentation. Think about it for a while. Is the message one that has true substance? Does it include the whole story? Read and study what the Bible has to say about the topic.

Next, spend the time, preferably in a quiet or special place, reading, considering and contemplating all you have studied. For many (including me), the hardest part is next. Write your thoughts down. Then, if you are comfortable with the dictation features or apps on many smart phones and other electronic devices, dictate your thoughts and let your thoughts appear in voice and in writing. If not, read your written thoughts out loud. When I do this, I am often amazed that what sounded so good and logical in my mind does not seem so good when I actually hear myself speak it out loud.

It also never hurts to talk these thoughts over with God. God hears better than any of us. I bet some additional thoughts will appear!

The end result of this "study" will nearly always be useful and helpful. It builds upon the reading of the Bible and gives us time to open our hearts and minds to a fuller understanding.

Discussion:

1. What are your "study" habits when trying to find an answer or solution to a problem?
2. How much time, if any, do you set aside each day or week for "study"?
3. When and where do you "study"?
4. If you are comfortable, describe examples of time when "study" has helped you find an answer.

Notes

Tool 3: Listen and hear

If I have followed the steps outlined above and have "listened," I am ready to "hear." What do I mean by "listen and hear"? I can sit and listen to a speech that sounds good. Then, the next day, I find it hard to recall what the speaker said. I bet many have had the same experience. I "listened" but did not "hear." Listening and hearing requires more effort. It requires the study we just talked about. Consciously recall and focus your memory on the important points you want to better understand and remember. Talk about these thoughts with others, if possible. Then, think some more.

Listening coupled with hearing can lead to true enhanced understanding, which fosters and underpins true faith. Yes, I said "enhanced" understanding. We are not expected to, nor will we ever, fully understand or have our work completed until the day of Christ's return.

Nevertheless, our understanding will grow. Paul makes this clear in Colossians 1:9–10:

> [9] For this reason, since the day we heard it, we have not ceased praying for you and asking that you may be filled with the knowledge of God's will in all spiritual wisdom and understanding, [10] so that you may lead lives worthy of the Lord, fully pleasing to him, as you bear fruit in every good work and as you grow in the knowledge of God.

Our work, no matter how good, is not done until Christ returns.

Philippians 1:6:

> [6] I am confident of this, that the one who began a good work among you will bring it to completion by the day of Jesus Christ.

And, remember, only the Lord has full understanding. Isaiah 40:28:

> [28] Do you not know? Have you not heard? The LORD is the everlasting God, the Creator of the ends of the earth. He will not grow tired or weary, and his understanding no one can fathom.

With this knowledge, when I have done my best to listen to the results of my reading and study and have made up my own mind about what I heard, a comfort can appear within me that makes all this not so mysterious and worrisome. Mother Teresa is credited with having said: "I have never had clarity, what I have always had is trust." She is right. The ups and downs of life can happen. Through faith and the trust that radiates from it, it will work out because God is in control. God has nothing but good in the plans for all that believe and try their best. Yes, when we each listen to the beating of our heart and truly hear God's word in the quiet and comfort of believing, faith manifests in us.

Romans 10:17:

> [17] So faith comes from hearing, and hearing through the word of Christ.

There is even more. "Hearing" is not the end of our work. James 1:22–25 makes it clear:

> [22] But be doers of the word, and not merely hearers who deceive themselves. [23] For if any are hearers of the word and not doers, they are like those who look at themselves in a mirror; [24] for they look at themselves and, ongoing away, immediately forget what they were like. [25] But those who look into the perfect law, the law of liberty, and persevere, being not hearers who forget but doers who act—they will be blessed in their doing.

And, in a sentence that I heard for many years before I felt I understood:
James 2:17:

> [17] So, faith by itself, if it has no works, is dead
> . . .

True faith manifests itself in our actions, which lead to good works. It is pretty simple. Works and faith are intertwined.

It is important to be a hearer of the word. One must hear before one can learn, understand and then "do." But those who hear and never progress can be the source of problems for themselves and for others. The "doing" confirms the Word and leads to the joy of living in faith! When we have *listened and heard*, and faith has firmly planted itself within our minds and hearts, it can grow by doing, and growing and doing, and on and on. (See Cardinal Step 6 for more on this.)

Discussion:

1. Describe and discuss when and how you have grown in your faith in the past.
2. Discuss where and how you would like to grow in your faith in the future.
3. Look over the list you are creating. Now, add your thoughts on opportunities for fun and growth by doing and giving that you see as possibilities for your future. Discuss with others your list if you are comfortable. Do any ideas from others give you new thoughts for your list?
4. Put down the list. Come back to it later, and again, and again. Does it grow or change as you read, study and think about it?

Notes

Chapter Five

Cardinal Step 4: Develop alternatives

The cardinal was about out of alternatives in the snowstorm. The purpose of working through this set of steps is to find alternatives while we have them— sometimes more than we even would guess. If we keep sitting on the branch, we may get lucky, and someone will come along with some of that food of life. But what if that does not happen? We can avoid falling into the cold of depression and even despair by acting now. Here are some thoughts for consideration.

Seek, through prayer, ideas and alternatives to consider.

How should we go about furthering the process of developing ideas and alternatives for our future? The place to start is in prayer. It is sometimes hard to know what to say or how to start. Is there something formal I need to do to be worthy to God's ears?

No, absolutely not! Most of us are accustomed to feeling inadequate or unwelcome to meet and visit with many a perceived powerful person. Nevertheless, think of how many problems of our world might have been solved if individuals had taken the opportunity to truly talk to those in positions of earthly power to impact daily life events. What if my boss knew my problem of working on a day when a child was sick with no alternative for care? Or knew that I stayed up all night with that sick child? What if someone up the line at work knew my car broke down on the morning of an important meeting? Does the minister at my church have time to talk to me about feelings of loneliness when others seem to have worse problems? Do government leaders have time to talk directly with everyone?

In most instances, our leaders do care and would like to talk to everyone in need—if there was just enough time. But, realistically, there are not enough hours in the day to talk with everyone. There is one, and only one, that has infinite time to talk directly with every single one of us. Moreover, we are assured in Philippians 4:6–7:

> [6] Do not worry about anything, but in everything by prayer and supplication with thanksgiving let your requests be made known to God. [7] And the peace of God, which surpasses all understanding, will guard your hearts and your minds in Christ Jesus.

Yes, there is no need to worry, though that may be easier said than done. Start by giving thanks to God for always being ready to listen. Then, make "known to God" what you need. Indeed, we are encouraged and have an open invitation to talk with God any time. That talk with God can open up ways never considered for solutions and comfort for problems.

Remember, there is more to prayer than asking for things. It is the opportunity to, in your own way and words, see what God thinks about things you are worrying about.

God has open arms for us and wants a personal relationship with us. One where we can engage in a special conversation with God. These talks with God have been in God's plan for us since the beginning.

John 1:1 starts:

> [1] In the beginning was the Word, and the Word was with God, and the Word was God.

Since the earliest English translations of the Bible, the Greek word "Logos," as used in John 1, has been translated as "the Word." Most scholars interpret "the Word" to refer to "Christ;" I agree. The relational and language-based nature of "Logos" when translated to English as "the Word" is uniquely enlightening. "The Word" is Christ. God, in referring to Christ in this way, intended—from the very beginning—to create a steadfast communication through Christ directly with every one of us. See Cardinal Step 5 (A)(2) below for more on the significance of the identification in John 1 of the "Word."

This is further confirmed in Genesis where Abraham's "talk" with God is recorded at Genesis 17:22:

> [22]And when he had finished talking with him, God went up from Abraham.

We also know that Moses talked with God when he received the Ten Commandments in Exodus 34:29:

> [29] Moses came down from Mount Sinai. As he came down from the mountain with the two tablets of the covenant in his hand, Moses did not know that the skin of his face shone because he had been <u>talking with God</u>.

Moreover, not only Abraham and Moses, but ordinary persons are promised a personal relationship with God. Luke 11:9–10 is so comforting in this regard. It confirms this relationship for everyone:

> [9] So, I say to you, ask, and it will be given to you; search, and you will find; knock, and the door will be opened for you. [10] For everyone who asks receives, and everyone who searches finds, and for everyone who knocks, the door will be opened.

The door is always open, and the direct relationship will be there to the end of time. Revelations 3:20 confirms:

> [20] Listen! I am standing at the door, knocking; if you hear my voice and open the door, I will come into you and eat with you, and you with me.

There is a bit more. Luke 11:1 describes what Jesus said when "one of his disciples said to him, 'Lord, teach us to pray, as John taught his disciples.'" And Jesus said to pray what we know as "The Lord's Prayer." Reciting and thinking about the words of the Lord's Prayer as a beginning to a talk with God feels comfortable to me. It is not a necessary part of every prayer, but I take comfort in its precise, all-encompassing message to God.

Just as we talk and enjoy the company and conversation with others over a meal, we truly can talk with God with our questions, cares, concerns, successes and failures. Billy Graham summed it up in simple straightforward eloquence:

> The Bible says, "Let us then approach the throne of grace with confidence, so that we may receive mercy and find grace to help us in our time of need" (Hebrews 4:16). If you have never done so, ask Christ to come into your life today. Then understand that God now welcomes you into His presence and promises to hear you—and He cannot lie. The Bible says, "This is the confidence we have in approaching God: that if we ask anything according to his will, he hears us" (1 John 5:14). Trust His promises and learn to bring every concern to Him in prayer.

For years when thinking about talking with God, my next thought was: How does this talk work? Will I get an answer? If so, how will I know it?

Yes, we will get answers. The very act of talking with God may cause us to see or know the answer without ever "hearing" it. For example, sometimes, articulating in silence thoughts with God results in my seeing that what was so concerning was not really as serious a problem as it seemed a few minutes ago. Some people believe they have heard God's voice. I have not and actually do not expect that. But, I have experienced what I believe was an answer in a feeling of relief and of a weight lifted from my shoulders when talking with God about concerns. An answer may appear later and so subtly that we do not recognize it as God's response.

A Garth Brooks song named "Unanswered Prayers" includes the line: "Some of God's greatest gifts are unanswered prayers." How many times have you thought something was so important only to find some time later it is not what you wanted or needed after all? I can recall years ago praying our offer would be accepted on a new home, only to feel devastated when someone outbid us. Then a few weeks later the opportunity to buy a home in a small community came along, and we have lived and loved life there ever since. God was answering, I just did not know it. I often think of another line in that Garth Brooks song that says it all for me: "because He doesn't answer doesn't mean He don't care."

God wants us to ask anything, anytime with the confidence of knowing that God cares, hears and will answer. There is nothing too trivial to talk to God about. To reiterate, read 1 John 5:14:

> [14] This is the confidence we have in approaching God: that if we ask anything according to his will, he hears us.

And remember, "patience is a virtue." That is an often-over-used saying. But oh, how true it is. God's "time" is worth waiting for. Paul, in his letter to the Romans, sums it up so very concisely:

Romans 12:12:

> [12] Rejoice in hope, be patient in suffering, persevere in prayer.

Pray every day and more often if you feel it. *Ask* and God will help you know when ideas and thoughts for the new and fulfilled future are real and for you.

Discussion:

1. What have you thought you needed *now* that, later, it was not nearly so important or needed?
2. Identify some examples of patience paying off in your life. In the lives of others.
3. Think about your prayers. Are you often rushed? Are you, at times, saying the words without really thinking about what you are asking or saying to God?
4. How could you make a talk with God more meaningful and comforting?
5. Have you ever talked over with God your thoughts and ideas about things you are trying to decide? What are some examples? Looking back now, did you find alternatives?

Notes

Seek, through prayer, ideas and alternatives to consider. Get yourself "right with..."

The alternative development process will more likely lead to the kind of future you are seeking if you are "right with..." The phrase has no ending because being "right with..." can have many contexts. Of course, the most important, and really only one in the end, is to be right with God. But to get there, the focus may need to start elsewhere. It starts with working on being "right with" yourself. From there, being "right with" others becomes much easier. Then one is ready to feel the warmth of a relationship that is "right with" God. You may also fill in the blank with other things, problems or issues that are dragging you down. But, in the end, do your best to get and be "right with your God."

Let's talk about this further.

(A) "Right with yourself"

As Jesus said when asked by a scribe in Mark 12:28–31:

> [28] "... Which commandment is the first of all?"
> [29] Jesus answered, "The first is, 'Hear, O Israel: the Lord our God, the Lord is one; [30] you shall love the Lord your God with all your heart, and with all your soul, and with all your mind, and with all your strength.' [31] The second is this, 'You shall love your neighbor as yourself.'

There is no other commandment greater than these."

The sentence "Love your neighbor as yourself" appears many other places in the Bible (you can search them out when answering the questions below). It is difficult to understand and thus follow this "second" and "equally important" commandment without loving yourself. Our relationship with the world generally grows from the relationship we have with ourselves. By that I mean, do I respect myself? Do I treat myself with care and have respect for the wonder of my existence? Am I proud of most of the decisions I make? Am I genuinely working at making good decisions?

None of us are perfect. We all may make decisions that are good, bad and various shades of right and wrong. That is just a part of nearly everyone's life. Remember, even negative decisions and actions that cannot be undone can have a positive result in the long run. We can learn from them and try not to make the same ones again, or over and over and over.

This is why I suggest first addressing and thinking about "love" of self. A right relationship with our own place in the world and with our feelings of self-worth and self-respect lead to the place we seek. If problems in this area are weighing on us, getting out and onward and upward may seem hard or even insurmountable to overcome. There are counselors, physicians and even friends and others who are very good at helping with solving these issues. There is the place to start. Get some professional or skilled help if you are having trouble finding "okay" or "alright" on your own.

Our focus in this little book is getting "right" with ourselves when things are "alright" but we just know we can do more. There is more wonder in store in the future!

Ponder this for a while—Do I truly love myself?

How do I determine that? First, loving oneself can be harmful if considered in the wrong context. Consider these Biblical truths and admonitions:

2 Timothy 3:1–2:

> [1] You must realize, however, that in the last days difficult times will come. [2] People will be: lovers of themselves, lovers of money, boastful, arrogant, abusive, disobedient to their parents, ungrateful, unholy.

Do any of these apply to you? Be truthful with yourself. No one else (but God) will know what you are thinking, and God is there to help.

Philippians 2:3:

> [3] Do nothing out of rivalry or conceit, but in humility consider others as more important than yourselves.

Can you do that? Can you keep it up and apply it every day?

And then look at Galatians 5:26:

> [26] Let us not become boastful, challenging one another, envying one another.

Again, this is an everyday admonition!
Finally, remember Psalm 139:14:

> [14] I will give thanks to you because I have been so amazingly and miraculously made. Your works are miraculous, and my soul is fully aware of this.

Recognize and give thanks every day for God's making you a part of creation. A miraculous awesome creation—you.

There are many more verses that make the same or similar points. For our purposes here, these verses are enough. They pointedly force us to examine what we "know" but may not be willing to confront. There is a state of living that can be harmful and is actually a false love of oneself. Each of us is a miracle of God's creation just as we are.

Arrogance, love of money, abusive behavior, lack of respect for the lives of others, ungratefulness for the things God has provided and actions we "know" deep down, at least, are unholy get us absolutely *nowhere*. When we understand this and focus on removing these actions and this "nowhere" direction from our lives, we will find a future that will be meaningful and fulfilling. Proverbs 22:1–2 addresses this and clearly describes a path onward and upward:

> [1] A good name is to be chosen rather than great riches, and favor is better than silver or gold. [2] The rich and the poor have this in common: the LORD is the maker of them all.

Money and net worth are never a substitute for a good name and the respect of others. We "know" this, but sometimes have to be reminded of it. We all have the same maker and wealth means nothing when seeking true happiness and that "heaven on earth." Of course, there is a level of subsistence that is necessary. Otherwise, these very basic needs can overwhelm our senses. It is, unfortunately, a state some people find themselves in, and there is different help needed from many sources. We are talking here about those with a level of basic needs met.

Proverbs 27:17–24 goes further:

> [17] Iron sharpens iron, and one person sharpens the wits of another...
> [19] Just as water reflects the face, so one human heart reflects another...
> [23] Know well the condition of your flocks, and give attention to your herds;
> [24] for riches do not last forever, nor a crown for all generations.

We are interconnected. We are all better ("sharpened") when we love and interact positively with one another. Riches and power do not last, but reflections of the heart do!

Finally, for today at least, Proverbs 19:8 says:

[8] To acquire wisdom is to love oneself; people who cherish understanding will prosper.

Prayer study and learning and listening, as we have discussed, lead to wisdom in which we will prosper. This is the wisdom of getting right with ourselves and understanding where we are and letting God lead us to our next step in life on earth. We will prosper in his light and not in the haze of a self-centered, non-listening life.

How we can leave a self-centered life? Does this mean we give up everything and start over? No, we can use what we have for good.

Spend some time on a regular basis thinking and praying about what has worked and what has not. Ask God for help getting "right with" yourself. Talk over how you can do that. Ask for help with alternative ideas and talk those over in prayer. Talk with friends and others you know that might be helpful, if you are comfortable. The guidance and ideas you seek will appear. Keep it up and that "self" you are seeking will also appear!

Keep in mind, many things follow a pattern a bit like the thoughts of Albert Einstein concerning invention that we discussed earlier in Chapter 1. Hitting upon something that works for you can be the result of the serendipity of life. A thought just pops into your mind that makes sense. A thoughtful search similarly sometimes hits upon a new idea. Hopefully, following the Cardinal Steps will stimulate more good thoughts. Building upon all these thoughts and efforts can create a surprisingly logical and now doable progression of advances in this adventure of life.

Discussion:

1. How can you or did you get to a place of feeling comfortable where you are?
2. How can you build upon good results from your past?
3. What have you observed others do that seems to have worked for them? Would that be something for you to try?
4. Go to a website like BibleGateway.com and search for the phrase "Love your neighbor as yourself." How many places is it found in the English Bible? Go to several translations and see if the number of citations varies. Why does it appear so many times? What are the contexts in which it appears?
5. As a practical matter, discuss how the admonition "Love your neighbor as yourself" can manifest itself in your everyday life.

Notes

Now, let's talk about how we get "right with others."

(B) "Right with others"

It is not so hard to find a way to get "right with others" if we have worked on understanding and becoming "right with ourselves." The not uncommon human temptation for self-promotion is then not nearly so compelling. Yes, many of our problems with others start with an effort to promote ourselves in the eyes of another. Moreover, many hurtful comments can be made in a knowing or, maybe, subconscious effort to reduce another to our level.

Even more harmful to being "right with others" is a drive for personal financial gain. Many are left in the wake of those who forget or intentionally push others out of the way in a climb to what is perceived to be the "top." Can you think of persons who appear to think little, if any, about others or those less fortunate? They can, and often do, fall hard from their perch. The Lord made every one of us and played no favorites. Monetary and physical riches are sometimes shockingly fragile. They may not last a lifetime. I am certain none of those things last into eternity!

Another problem is most of those trampled in the process of a never-ending drive for personal gain never forget. This is not just true in the short term. Look at the world and think about the retribution sought today for things that occurred to ancestors hundreds or even thousands of years ago. It takes someone willing to break that progression, especially early on, for the cycle to end. True love of our neighbors and acting upon that love is where the end of that cycle begins. Make yourself the beginning.

Jesus gave us the formula in 2 Peter 1:3–11:

> [3] His divine power has given us everything needed for life and godliness, through the knowledge of him who called us by his own glory and goodness. [4] Thus he has given us, through these things, his precious and very great promises, so that through them you may escape from the corruption that is in the world because of lust, and may become participants of the divine nature. [5] <u>For this very reason, you must make every effort to support your faith with goodness, and goodness with knowledge,</u> [6] <u>and knowledge with self-control, and self-control with endurance, and endurance with godliness,</u> [7] <u>and godliness with mutual affection, and mutual affection with love.</u> [8] For if these things are yours and are increasing among you, they keep you from being ineffective and unfruitful in the knowledge of our Lord Jesus Christ. [9] For anyone who lacks these things is short-sighted and blind, and is forgetful of the cleansing of past sins. [10] Therefore, brothers and sisters, be all the more eager to confirm your call and election, for if you do this, you will never stumble. [11] For in this way, entry into the eternal kingdom of our Lord and Savior Jesus Christ will be richly provided for you.

Think about it. Supporting your faith with goodness leads to knowledge which leads to wisdom and, ultimately, a life we seek. One of mutual affection and love of one another.

So, just relax and remember these things. God made you. Christ died for our sins. God grants forgiveness through grace. Removing from our focus what we know is "unholy" clears the way to forgiveness, wisdom and the true resulting prosperity of life in faith. (Not exactly what some may think of when focusing only on "prospering" by acquiring for ourselves more and more money or "things.")

Paul's letters to the Thessalonians are helpful to consider here. Paul tells the Thessalonians at 1 Thessalonians 5:15:

[15] See that none of you repays evil for evil, but always seek to do good to one another and to all.

Leave revenge and vengeance to God. Only God knows the full story from the other side and will act, if needed. Paul makes this clear in 2 Thessalonians 1:6:

[6] For it is indeed just of God to repay with affliction those who afflict you…

It is then up to us to do one of the hardest things we are asked to do: "forgive and forget." If we are bold enough to do this, nothing from our past will drag us down. Suddenly, we are free! Free to follow God's direction as recorded in Mathew 5:44:

^{44} …love your enemies and pray for those who persecute you.

Most, including me for sure, find this hard to do. But I believe steadfastly working at following these principles will bring the joy and peace only one in Christ can know.

One more set of thoughts while we are here. Proverbs 27:17,19 is so true:

> ^{17} Iron sharpens iron, and one person sharpens the wits of another…
> ^{19} Just as water reflects the face, so one human heart reflects another.

We are all in this together. Working with and for each other is the way to the life we seek.

Ephesians 4:11–13 sums it up:

> ^{11} So, Christ himself gave the apostles, the prophets, the evangelists, the pastors and teachers, ^{12} to equip his people for works of service, so that the body of Christ may be built up ^{13} until we all reach unity in the faith and in the knowledge of the Son of God and become mature, attaining to the whole measure of the fullness of Christ.

We are builders, servers, teachers and/or leaders of or for someone else. It all started with our God in heaven, was manifested on earth in Christ and continues here on earth through each person walking in the Holy

Spirit. Hopefully, truth, honor and love of our fellow humans, if made a way of life by more and more, will rub off on those we touch in daily life and after a time the world will be a better place. I know this all sounds like preaching—and I guess it actually is. But this is so important to think about. It may seem too idealistic—but I do not think so. Not if the synergies created by more and more people's actions take hold first on my "street," then in my "town" and on and on.

Discussion:

1. What can each of us do to better get "right with others" and stay there?
2. How would one go about mitigating a perceived "wrong" to another?
3. How would one go about forgiving the wrong of another?

Notes

Now, we are ready to discuss the most important of these "getting right" discussions—"right with God."

(C) "Right with God"

The Merriam-Webster dictionary defines righteous, when referring to a personal action or conduct, as "morally right or justifiable." An internet search finds the word "righteous" used in English translations of the Bible over five hundred times. These biblical uses set an even higher bar. In 2 Corinthians 5:20–21 we find:

> [20] So we are ambassadors for Christ, since God is making his appeal through us; we entreat you on behalf of Christ, be reconciled to God. [21] For our sake he made him to be sin who knew no sin, so that in him we might become the righteousness of God.

Becoming the "righteousness of God" is a seemingly impossible task. And it would be if it were not for the grace of God and the sacrifice of Jesus for us. Those who have true faith in God, that acknowledge their sins and that ask forgiveness are forgiven and can achieve the righteousness of God by the sacrifice of Christ. The getting "right with God" that I am talking about is working for and living in that righteousness.

Many, maybe most, of the actions or inactions that place us without God involve our actions to, toward or with others. God knows what we "know," what we do, what we have done and what we are thinking about doing. Very intimidating—but also comforting, in perhaps an unexpected way. If I am working at being right with myself and others, God knows I am working in Christ's light and doing my best to follow a path God has for me. One that will lead me into the right and light of forgiveness and peace.

It is also important to remember, God knows we are not perfect. I suggest we also just "know" when we have done something that is not right. This is especially true when it comes to the things that leave us not "right with" God. We can make excuses to ourselves all day long, but we "know" where we stand. It is when we admit the wrong to ourselves and truly ask God's forgiveness that, through God's grace, we can get, be and stay "right" with our God.

This takes self-discipline and, even more so, a heavy dose of perseverance to get right and stay right. Most of us will fall short from time to time. But I suggest we periodically take stock of where we stand and "clear the decks" of the burdens and baggage that may have appeared in our lives since the last "deck clearing." If we are progressing in our faith journey, there should be less to clear each time we undertake the effort. It can be amazingly comforting when I know that God is with me and will guide me toward more "right" decisions from now on.

Psalm 32:8 confirms:

> [8] I will instruct you and teach you the way you should go; I will counsel you with my eye upon you.

Being "right with God" does not mean we have become infallible and have achieved perfectly the "righteousness of God." It does mean we are genuinely and faithfully working on living in and serving in the righteousness of God and asking every day for God's help and counsel.

(D) Fulfilment!

When one is living in a way that seeks through prayers and action to be right with ourselves, others and God, good things just happen! Fulfillment of the promise of heaven on earth may not be far away; it is time to finalize your list of ideas and alternatives. Just doing this should be fulfilling. It will take time and effort to genuinely work your way through each of these steps.

Spend whatever time is necessary to go back through your notes and pull out the thoughts and points that help you create a list of realistic alternative actions. After it is created, put it aside and come back to it later. Think it through again. Add anything new that you identify. Be sure you have taken the time to dream a bit. Include an item or two that may seem pretty far out. Time and situations change. It might not be unrealistic in the future. It can also be a starting place when you pick up with this exercise again in the future.

Congratulations! You are now ready to do some real good! It will be fun to see where the implementation of these alternatives leads.

Discussion:

1. Give some examples where you have experienced good things just happening.
2. Give some examples where you have seen good things just happen for others.
3. Describe a time you felt you received counsel from God.
4. Describe a time when you just knew God was there for you.
5. List alternatives you can identify that are things you can realistically do for your future.
6. Now dream a little, and list things you would like to do that seem out of reach now but, maybe not, if things work out.

Notes

Chapter Six

Cardinal Step 5: Test or try alternatives

God created the cardinal and, over time, it has evolved traits that help it survive and grow. It has that ability to fluff up and also, in extreme cold, will shiver, which generates warmth inside that bundle of fluffy feathers. It generally eats insects, worms and seeds on the ground. But it will eat from a perch on a feeder when necessary.

God created us with the awesome and unique ability to react to circumstances and adapt to our environment and situations quickly. We can try new things, learn from them, make changes and move forward.

Alternatives are just that—alternatives. Not all will work out. But some will! A few more thoughts may be helpful.

Plant some trees

I have often repeated something I heard a country preacher say at a funeral that I thought was so true about the person being eulogized.

The statement was to the effect of: "A life that plants some trees under whose shade the person will never rest has created a wonderful legacy." I have since found that history has not clearly recorded where that thought originated. Some believe it was a product of an anonymous ancient Greek proverb which has been quoted as, "Society grows great when old men plant trees whose shade they know they shall never sit in." Wherever it originated, that preacher hit the nail on the head when he used it to describe the life being praised.

We do many things at different times in our lives, and we may never know how things turned out. But that is beside the true point. The development of the alternatives we have identified is founded in gratitude for the many wonderful things that God has provided to us. Marcus Tullius Cicero is often noted as having said in the ancient Roman world, "Gratitude is not only the greatest of virtues, but the parent of all the others."

Being thankful for the gifts we have been given, and acting in that light, leads to many more good deeds and things that can make our world a better place. Moreover, good and great comfort and cheer can spring from that perpetual, full throttle, grateful giving to and for others. Along that line, consider 2 Corinthians 9:6–7:

> [6] The point is this: the one who sows sparingly will also reap sparingly, and the one who sows bountifully will also reap bountifully. [7] Each of you must give as you have made up your mind, not reluctantly or under compulsion, for God loves a cheerful giver.

God is saying give, give freely and give cheerfully. If we do, we will be amazed at the bounty of good that will come not only to the lives of others but to our lives as well. And, maybe, many times over. This does not mean that this bounty will be monetary at all. Rather, it is focused on something much more important and fulfilling: the good feeling of a life well lived.

(A) Some additional things to keep in mind while doing the work of "planting":

   (1) Take heed—good cheer is not always free. Planting those trees may require personal sacrifice. Luke 21:1–4 is one of my favorites of the many parables Jesus related. It is about "The Widow's Two Mites":

> [1] And He looked up and saw the rich putting their gifts into the treasury, [2] and He saw also a certain poor widow putting in two mites. [3] So He said, "Truly I say to you that this poor widow has put in more than all; [4] for all these out of their abundance have put in offerings for God, but she out of her poverty put in all the livelihood that she had."

The widow made a dramatic, real sacrifice for the good of others in need. Ask yourself: Am I willing to really sacrifice for the good of others?

   (2) It is not always easy to step out of our comfort zone to help others. It can be terrifying to raise up and expose ourselves to the criticism, mean

comments, condescending thoughts and posts that seem so prevalent in today's electronic commentary world. People today are willing to say things in electronic print that would never be said face-to-face. Do not become trapped or caught up in that world. Talk to others as you would talk with them face-to-face. Indeed, as we discussed earlier, the Book of John starts (1:1–5):

> [1] In the beginning was the Word, and the Word was with God, and the Word was God. [2] He was in the beginning with God. [3] All things came into being through him, and without him not one thing came into being. What has come into being [4] in him was life, and the life was the light of all people. [5] The light shines in the darkness, and the darkness did not overcome it.

The term "Logos", translated into English as "Word", focuses my attention upon God's speaking creation into existence. The Word already existed at creation. God spoke creation into existence and gave us not only the ability to use words, but also the opportunity to become a part of the Word through the Holy Spirit. We must take care in how we use this God-given power in speaking to others in person, electronically or in writing. Damage can be done to others with hurtful words. Many physical injuries will heal over time. Words can be carried in the memory forever. I recall to this day hurtful words spoken to and about me many years ago. I bet many of you can think of those events in your past as well. The occurrence hurt my feelings, did not change anything and certainly did not help my feelings about the speaker. I have forgiven, but forgetting has been more difficult. Stopping the use of verbal assaults, rumors and other hurtful words will change the speaker's life and the lives of those that might be the targets of those words. Let the Holy Spirit guide the use of the God-given gift of language.

(3) On the other side of this "word" discussion is the use of words to reward, acknowledge, praise and positively lead others. A smile accompanying these words never hurts as well. I can, and I bet you can also, remember some positive words that were received that still warm my heart and even guide my thoughts today. Jesus told the parable of the mustard seed in Mathew 13:31–32:

> [31] He put before them another parable: "The kingdom of heaven is like a mustard seed that someone took and sowed in his field; [32] it is the smallest of all the seeds, but when it has grown it is the greatest of shrubs and becomes a tree, so that the birds of the air come and make nests in its branches."

Some years ago, op-ed columnist, Pulitzer Prize winning writer and best-selling author

Thomas Friedman spoke at a dinner that my wife and I attended.

He made any number of points, and the one I found most compelling related to humiliation and dignity. He stated that, in his opinion, the two most compelling human emotions are just those—humiliation and dignity. I agree. In all our use of "words," those that humiliate never have positive results and can never be undone, especially if put in writing on social media or print. *But,* those "words" that show respect and cause others to know and feel dignity can have miraculous results. Make yourself the giver of kind and encouraging words. Those little "mustard seed" words will grow into a tree with strong and nesting branches of life for all.

(4) Another parable, Mathew 13:29–30, is helpful:

> [29] But he replied, "No; for in gathering the weeds you would uproot the wheat along with them. [30] Let both of them grow together until the harvest; and at harvest time I will tell the reapers, 'Collect the weeds first and bind them in bundles to be burned, but gather the wheat into my barn.'"

One of the first steps to finding joy and true happiness in life is to step out; don't be afraid to get down in those weeds and look for the good that will bear fruit. There will be some weeds to bundle and sort through. This very process is how we can many times stumble onto what we are seeking!

On the morning of writing this, I attended the Palm Sunday service at my home church, Westminster Presbyterian Church in Oklahoma City. Rev. Landon Whitsitt incorporates a children's time early in each service. The children are invited to the chancel steps near the beginning of the service, and they run to the front and fill the steps. Rev. Whitsitt tells a short summary of the Bible verse or story for the service. It is sometimes dramatic and always in plain kid language. (I am not sure who learns more from it, me or the kids.) The children then leave with teachers for their own service in the church chapel. This Sunday, the lesson was Luke 9:28–40. It includes the story of how two of the disciples were asked by Jesus to go into the village, where they would find tied there a colt (donkey). He asked that they untie it and bring it to him. Jesus then said, "If anyone asks you, 'Why are you untying it?' just say 'The Lord needs it.'"

Rev. Whitsitt usually asks the children a question or questions that they will discuss later in their service. This morning he asked: "What would you do if this was your donkey and two men untied it?" One child blurted out "I would give it to them if Jesus needed it!"

What an example of the spontaneous and powerful thoughts of a child! As I thought about it, I realized there is much more than the obvious in that answer. We many times struggle with how to determine which are the weeds and which is the wheat as we look at the opportunities of life in our future. It became even clearer to me that is how we find the "wheat"—the bread that will feed our future. We must ask ourselves as we consider the list of alternatives we are creating, "Would Jesus ask me to do it?" If we ask ourselves that question and hear in our inner thoughts the answer is "Yes, if Jesus needs it," we are on the right track. But, keep in mind, following the law is also one of our admonitions.

Romans 13:1–5 (being subject to authorities):

> [1] Let every person be subject to the governing authorities, for there is no authority except from God, and those authorities that exist have been instituted by God. [2] Therefore whoever resists authority resists what God has appointed, and those who resist will incur judgment. [3] For rulers are not a terror to good conduct but to bad. Do you wish to have no fear of the authority? Then do what is good, and you will receive its approval, [4] for it is God's agent for your good. But if you do what is wrong, you should be afraid, for the authority does not bear the sword in

vain! It is the agent of God to execute wrath on the wrongdoer. [5] Therefore one must be subject, not only because of wrath but also because of conscience.

We cannot blindly do what we *believe* is God's will. We must use our God-given judgement in determining our own behavior.

(5) And finally, self-fulfillment. A question that is constantly at play when "planting" for the future is: "What are my gifts?" Many "creators" take great pleasure and personal satisfaction in the act of creating a painting, a song, a photograph, a woodworking project and any one of many other creations of mental and physical skills. This, in fact, may be all one needs to find fulfillment. Similarly, for some, reading to be an informed person is fulfilling. Others may read history and contemplate and find it fulfilling to contemplate and discuss with others the lessons to be learned from it. I am suggesting that if one finds peace and fulfillment from these activities alone, that is good. Moreover, if that inner peace permeates the person's life in this world with others, it can rub off. God's world becomes a better place for us all to live. What more could God expect of us? Then, many may know that feeling of "heaven on earth."

When I was a college student, I got a summer job working as an intern at a large aircraft repair facility about thirty miles from my home. One of our neighbors was my parents' age and worked in the aircraft shop full-time. He drove the thirty miles every day. For that summer, we car-shared rides to work. I learned from him that there is certainly a lot more to life than just money. He was not a high-paid worker. Many evenings after work, he was anxious to get home. He and, often, his wife or a friend, were going fishing. I believe he was as happy and contented as anyone I have known in all the years since.

This then-skinny kid with horned rim glasses learned and benefited forever in just being with him for that short interval. He was sharing with others everyday life and making a difference for others by his very nature!

A number of years ago, I travelled to Israel as a part of my work. While there, I joined for a day a group of leaders and involved citizens from Oklahoma City that were there on a special "get acquainted" trip. At that time, there was a tree planting initiative in certain parts of Israel. It is hoped that, over time, the initiative will help change the landscape. Several of us planted a seedling tree each at a drip point of plastic lines laid all across a hillside. Someday, I hope to return to the then-barren hillside and see what has happened to those little trees we planted.

On a later trip to Israel, our church group spent several days in Jerusalem, and we visited the Garden of Gethsemane. There are a number of olive trees growing today that are understood to have been there when Jesus walked the path through the Garden. I doubt the planters of those olive trees had any idea who would sit in the trees' shade, and that people would be enjoying their fruits and shade over two thousand years later.

One never knows what the simple act of planting can do—now and forever.

Discussion:

1. Again, what are your gifts—any new thoughts?
2. Where might you "plant" trees using these gifts?
3. Do you have possible gifts you would like to develop? What are they?
4. What are your alternatives? Which ones would Jesus ask you to do? Add to and finish your list.
5. How can you get started on one or more of these alternatives where "yes" is your answer?
6. How much will it cost? (What does this mean? Money? Time? Commitment? What else?)
7. Is there baggage from bad feelings etc. that need to be forgiven?
8. Do you really understand what there is to do? Do you need more information? What do you need to do to get the information? Do you need to work on your list some more?
9. Are there things for you to watch to determine whether you are finding the things you have hoped to find? Do you hear that "yes" echoing in your inner being?
10. What do you do if more than one alternative is yielding promising results?

Notes

Chapter Seven

Cardinal Step 6: Go for it!

Yes, go for it. You will see this chapter is shorter than the others. That is because it is now your turn to act and write your own Cardinal Step. Through trial and error, identify and act on the best alternative(s) you can realistically implement. Pick what you enjoy and is fulfilling and *go for it!* There are so many things that may be just what you have been looking for to bring back that energy and enthusiasm for the day and fulfilment of life you have been missing.

Take the one on the top of your list and take some action on it. My experience has been that the top item many times is not the answer. But, by working on it, the real answer will often appear. The Bible confirms this in Ecclesiastes 11:6:

> [6] In the morning sow your seed, and at evening do not let your hands be idle; for you do not know which will prosper, this or that, or whether both alike will be good.

Give your alternatives the chance to bear seed. One or more, and maybe even all, will provide you with an amazing future. Do not give up; stick with it until you get that feeling of fulfillment.

As age has crept up on me, I have come to realize that perhaps the most valuable thing I have is time. If I share it with others, and with God, doing what God would have me do, what more can I do in seeking fulfillment? Of course, money and physical things can make a real difference when given to others in need. But, for many, time is the hardest thing to give to others in today's world. When time and physical treasure are combined, the possibilities are endless.

Take the time needed to do whatever you choose "right." That may mean things take longer than you envisioned, but it will be worth it. There will likely be some bumps along the way. Keep it up and look for the successes. Focus on those and chalk up the losses to learning and know that is a part of the process.

We all know that runners, at times, get a feeling they call a "runners high." It appears after a time and carries a runner on to the end of a hard run. I believe that same type of feeling may appear when one helps a child understand a lesson they are struggling with for school, or one spends a day loading groceries for those in need, or talks with a friend about their struggles, or just talks with and enjoys the company of others, or prepares a meal for a neighbor, or advises about a startup business, or does handy work for one in need, or reads a book and shares it with others, and _____, and _____, and _____. You fill in the blanks! All the work of finding your future will pay off. You will know it and feel it. The heavenly light on earth will shine on more than just you and will last much longer than one run.

I recall being one of the grandfathers on an outing with my granddaughter's Girl Scout troop. We went to a mission where the girls helped prepare bags of things to be given to other children during their shopping for their parents for Christmas. The kids had a great time filling the bags for several hundred children. They giggled, talked and laughed. I heard one say above the crowd, "This is so much fun, let's do this every Saturday." That feeling of true happiness permeated that day for that girl, just like it did for her grandfather when he heard her say it.

On that same day, I observed another person there not nearly as fortunate as I have been from a financial standpoint. The little sister of one of the Scouts was shy and was holding back on participating, hiding behind her mother's leg. She was encouraged to take part and gradually moved up and got in the line and, before it was over, was one of the hardest working children there. As the work ended, one of the other grandfathers physically struggled to get up from his chair, walked over to the young girl and pulled out a coin. He gave it to the little child and said he wanted to give it to her because she deserved a reward for being such a hard worker. That coin, given to a child he did not know by one who probably had limited financial means, created a beam on that little girl's face—and on that grandfather's face. That day, I felt I saw the shining light of Christ reflecting from those faces.

Yes, it is time to go for it! That heaven on earth is there and everywhere if we look for it.

Discussion:

1. Identify some examples of that shining light you have seen. Discuss them and look for a pattern in the examples.
2. Select one of your alternatives and discuss it with others.
3. Repeat this with another alternative on your list.
4. Pick a starting point for trying the alternatives you have identified.
5. Write down the details of what you plan to do and check them off when they are: 1) started, 2) underway and 3) completed. Then go to the next one or more. (Nothing says you cannot do more than one at a time but, take care. Try to avoid overindulging or spreading yourself too thin. The result can be skewed by the overwork and be disappointing.) Encourage others on this adventure to do the same exercise. Then share what you would like with those that would also like to share.

Notes

Chapter Eight

A few more thoughts

We are not finished. Things do not always go as planned or hoped. The feelings of success, joy and fulfilment may come and go. I have a few more thoughts.

Persevere

Just as the cardinal had to sit on the limb and wait, action does not always translate to immediate success. In fact, in my experience, it is much more likely that success will take some time and there may be "stuff" that happens to interrupt or change the plan.

Harold Kushner's 2004 book *When Bad Things Happen To Good People* was almost immediately a best seller. I think this is because it focuses on one of the questions that people, no matter their economic or other situation in life or religious beliefs, have struggled to answer—probably since nearly the beginning of time. It is easy to decide that when bad things happen it is punishment for something. Did you ever search your mind for what you did wrong when something bad happened to you? Most of us have, and it can be easy to get bogged down in the personal search for "why."

One more comforting and supporting thought: God, through the Holy Spirit, fully dwells in and works with and through us. 1 Corinthians 3:16 dramatically states:

> [16] Don't you know that you yourselves are God's temple and God's Spirit dwells in your midst?

Yes, God's awesome power is at work within and with each of us. We have a huge responsibility to carefully and thoughtfully use that power for good purposes. But, what a relief! I do not have to do this all alone. The Holy Spirit is carrying me and will guide and lead me *if I let it.*

Discussion:

1. Think of a time when your plans or work were interrupted by an unexpected and difficult event, and you hung in there and got back to it later and it worked out as you hoped. How did that feel?
2. Do you have an example of such an occurrence where things worked out even better than you hoped?
3. How might failure affect you when trying an alternative that you thought was "it"?
4. What are some thoughts on how to overcome the feelings that accompany lack of success at an endeavor?

Notes

Boast not

That beautiful cardinal was fluffed up and was putting on quite an attention-getting show. We know it was not, though, and underneath it all, the fluff was keeping it warm in a potentially difficult situation. Unfortunately, at times, we "fluff up" and seek self-serving attention to benefit our ego and nothing more.

It is oh-so-easy to decide that success, and good luck for that matter, came because one is so outstanding and smart. One can think, "I have worked hard and have earned it." Upon careful reflection, which is not what happened at all. Success and good luck, whatever the source or cause, are gifts from God. Ask for God's help and guidance in using for good purposes the fruits of success and good luck.

Boasting and arrogance seldom work for those who exhibit or flaunt their self-decided "greatness" to others. This may make the boastful and arrogant person feel good temporarily, but it does not raise a person's standing in others' eyes and minds. Also, the reaction of some may be jealousy, and the negative effects of that can affect both the initiator and the receiver. Others may consciously or subconsciously copy the behavior. The initiator may end up teaching others to follow this downward life that often ends in disaster.

And another thing to keep in mind: If brotherly love permeates our lives, boasting about brotherly, loving acts can become a cloud over an otherwise beautiful day. Paul addresses exactly this in 1 Corinthians 4:7:

⁷ For who sees anything different in you? What do you have that you did not receive? And if you received it, why do you boast as if it were not a gift?

Paul succinctly addresses all of this in 1 Corinthians 13:4:

⁴ Love is patient; love is kind; love is not envious, boastful, or arrogant.

Yes, everything we have, including our very lives, is a gift from God. Thankfulness, devoid of boastfulness and arrogance, is the ticket for a ride on the train to heaven on earth.

Discussion:

1. Give some examples of brotherly love you have witnessed.
2. Give some examples of disasters that you have seen occur to the boastful.
3. Give some examples of disasters that you have seen occur to the arrogant.

Notes

Relax and be patient

Earlier in this book I mentioned a trip to Mexico many years ago. Beauty and the serenity of God's creation filled me for a short moment. I wish I had allowed for more of those moments as I marched through a busy everyday life.

I recently watched a scene of a 1952 movie I landed on while channel surfing. The characters in the scene complained and asked how they were to deal with all the changes in the world and the young people's new ideas. I could not help thinking that today those young people of 1952, now much older, would make the same complaints and have the same concerns when looking at today's young people. The "todays" become the "past" soon to be replaced by another "today."

What does that mean for us? The answer is simple. Look at Romans 8:25 and 27:

> [25] But if we hope for what we do not see, we wait for it with patience. [26] Likewise the Spirit helps us in our weakness; for we do not know how to pray as we ought, but that very Spirit intercedes with sighs too deep for words. [27] And God, who searches the heart, knows what the mind of the Spirit is, because the Spirit intercedes for the saints according to the will of God.

I take these verses to be telling me to be patient and the Spirit will guide me. The "hurry" or "the everchanging winds of life" (as I sometimes like to call the "hurry" phenomenon) does not have to define me. If I am patient and slow down a bit, the Holy Spirit will guide me and keep me whole and comforted.

John 3:8 reads:

> [8] The wind blows where it chooses, and you hear it, but you do not know where it comes from or where it goes. So it is with everyone who is born of the Spirit.

Think about it; have you ever heard the wind and wondered, where did it start? And where will those particles carried by the wind end up? (Those that do not end up on my porch anyway!) Our lives in Christ's time are similar. The effect of time on a patient life in Christ is something like a beautiful crystal, ever changing in the light. That light of the Spirit will shine differently on each of us today and tomorrow—and thus it goes as "tomorrows" become "todays"—ever brighter and fulfilling. If we share this comfort with those around us, the concerns of the past do not have to become a pattern of concerns forever.

Now, let us focus for another moment upon how we can break this chain of "concerns."

In my litigation law life, I found, to my great comfort, that most of the lawyers, business people, witnesses and others involved were good and honest persons. Many were "on the other side," yet they earned and deserved my respect. Some of my good friends today are those I opposed in hard-fought, high-stakes cases and very difficult situations.

But, then, to my great discomfort, there are the others. Those that have little or no concern for honesty and good faith. Name calling, verbal abuse, intimidation and worse are a way of life for them.

I have concluded, after many years in the fray, the best thing I can do is try to avoid being caught up in a "fighting fire with fire" response. And then avoid later seeking revenge, which only starts the cycle over again. Being unwilling to get caught in that trap can be astonishingly disarming to those verbal abusers. A seemed disadvantage becomes an advantage.

One of my favorite passages is 2 Peter 1:5–8, 10:

> [5] For this very reason, make every effort to add to your faith, goodness; and to goodness, knowledge; [6] and to knowledge, self-control; and to self-control, perseverance; and to perseverance, godliness; [7] and to godliness, mutual affection; and to mutual affection, love. [8] For if you possess these qualities in increasing measure, they will keep you from being ineffective and unproductive in your knowledge of our Lord Jesus Christ... [10] Therefore, my brothers and sisters, make every effort to confirm your calling and election. For if you do these things, you will never stumble, [11] and you will receive a rich welcome into the eternal kingdom of our Lord and Savior Jesus Christ.

If I am patient and listen, the Spirit will not only guide me but also re-center me. Galatians 5:22–23 is refreshingly straightforward:

> [22] …the fruit of the Spirit is love, joy, peace, patience, kindness, generosity, faithfulness, [23] gentleness, and self-control. There is no law against such things.

The Holy Spirit fully dwells within and works with and through each of us. 1 Corinthians 3:16 confirms again:

> [16] Don't you know that you yourselves are God's temple and God's Spirit dwells in your midst?

Wow, that means the awesome power is at work within and for me. It also means I have a huge responsibility—a heavy thought. I have a responsibility to be a home for it.

Moreover, the comfort that permeates a home in heaven with God can be here on earth, right now. I will know it when I see and feel it. The happiness that permeates the moments God provides, if I just take the time to listen, is there for me. Faith grows with each day. Living life to the fullest today with "love, joy, peace, patience, kindness, generosity, faithfulness, gentleness, and self-control" as my ceaseless goal and effort will make every day better than the last—forever! The concerns of the past can fade away and the next generations will each progress toward that comforting future we all seek.

Discussion:

1. How can you influence your future by "taking the time" today?
2. Be on the lookout next week for the awesome moments that are there. Take the time to enjoy and experience them. Write them down and describe them for others undertaking this experiential exercise.
3. Have you solved problems by following the admonitions of 2 Peter 1? How can you incorporate this approach to life in your future actions?
4. Think about your list of alternatives; did anything new appear?

Notes

Be thankful and express it

The gift of faith is exactly that—a gift from God. Through that faith, God's grace and salvation are there for everyone—*always*. We are a part of the body of Christ and are all in this life together. I hope we remember how wonderful that is and how much others do to make our world and lives better. I hope I will always give thanks to God and to those who are with us in our work and everyday lives. Most importantly, I hope I remember to thank those living a life of giving to and respecting and honoring others. Yes, that means every one of you! *Thank you for being you!*

Chapter Nine

Results

We are at the end of this exercise in the name of that beautiful but struggling cardinal. As we have gone along, I too have been recording my personal thoughts and ideas. This book has developed as I have worked on it—so has my personal list of "Cardinal Rules." I have also included a list of related thoughts that help guide me when confronted with those day-to-day decisions that can delay, confuse, obscure and cloud an otherwise "sunny" day. *And*, in one more effort to help make this useful for daily living, I have incorporated an example of the application of the Cardinal Steps to a common living life problem that some struggle with.

My Cardinal Rules

1. Until my last day here on earth, there is always more I can do. "Hope springs eternal!"
2. God is always there for me. I believe in God's grace and that God will forgive my missteps if I genuinely try my best to do better and sincerely and meaningfully ask for forgiveness. Yes, "hope springs eternal!"
3. Prayer is the vehicle to carry me along the way.
4. The Bible is my guidebook. It has an answer to all my questions about turns in the road if I take the time to search for them.

5. Action on my part makes the difference. If I try, not everything will work, but I will be a little better and ready for more each time I try.
6. I am successful if, gradually, I am no longer critical to a project's outcome. I will then have time to look for what is next!
7. I will make a difference not only in my life but, hopefully and most importantly, in the lives of others.
8. The trees I plant can grow and provide shade and comfort long after I am gone.
9. I will find my way—with God's help! Heaven on earth is achievable in ever-increasing measure.
10. The mystery of it all is mesmerizing and transformational. (We did not discuss this in detail. I will have more to say about this later…)

My Cardinal Rules are founded upon the simple and direct answer Jesus gave the scribe in the temple (Mark 12:30–31):

> [30] "[Y]ou shall love the Lord your God with all your heart, and with all your soul, and with all your mind, and with all your strength." [31] The second is this, "You shall love your neighbor as yourself." There is no other commandment greater than these.

My thoughts for guiding daily actions

One topic that sometimes comes up when I discuss the Cardinal Steps and ideas in this book relates to how these tools can be used in hurried daily life. We are not always needing to make life-changing decisions. We just want some help finding our way through the challenges and decisions that confront us and must be made today. If one has successfully worked their way through the Cardinal Steps, the principles will be familiar and may be readily useful. This is especially true if they are reviewed periodically. After or during each review, write down and keep somewhere easily accessible your own list of thoughts you think are most useful for day-to-day problem solving and decision making. Mine are:

1. Stop, relax, calm down and take at least a short time to think in a quiet place.
2. Be realistic. What is possible *today*? Address those issues. Bigger issues will work out— just give them time.
3. Take the time to make some notes; the act of typing or writing things down helps organize thoughts and sound out in your mind issues and options. Sometimes, the answer becomes clear without more.
4. Talk it over with your God—prayer always helps, even if it must be short.
5. Resist anger, lashing out, yelling or threatening. These actions seldom, if ever, help, and most often hurt.
6. Did I take the time to gather the information needed to make a good decision?
7. Ask: "Would Jesus ask me to do it?" "Will it not hurt someone else, physically and/or emotionally?"
8. Will God be okay with me if I do it?

If you have done 1–5 and the answer to 6–8 is "yes," go for it. The decision you make should be okay! It may not be perfect and may not always be right, but the risk of a wrong and harmful step is minimized. If you are not comfortable, take some more time. Most errors are made from acting too quickly.

An example

The Cardinal Steps we have been discussing can be applied to more than just a big-picture, life-direction change. At various times, most of us are confronted with decisions just as important but more focused on our individual personal situations. These can include the difficulties of dealing with getting older, career and job dilemmas and choices, events involving significant others or spouses, loss of a loved one, loneliness, family issues, health, dealing with difficult people and many other things. These personal situations can create the need for decision making now when alternatives are few or are not clear. They are somewhere in between the big picture decisions and the day-to-day decision-making dilemmas we have just discussed. The Cardinal Steps can help work through these decisions as well. As an example, let's take one of these issues and work our way through the application of the Cardinal Step process to it.

Loneliness is a problem that can raise its head at most any time in life. It can exist when one is surrounded by people or when home alone. It can occur to one person or a couple. It may not even be clear it is the problem. Stirring around doing routine things, doing things that are not enjoyed or fulfilling, overwork or other activities can mask loneliness. It can appear during the unexpected isolation of a pandemic. Health issues can bring it on.

Depression is often a product of loneliness and vice versa. I cannot overemphasize, when one thinks depression may be involved, professional counseling or medical advice can be very important. In fact, that should be considered as a part of this first Cardinal Step. Make sure there is not treatable depression that is causing or seriously contributing to lonely feelings.

Next, as a part of Cardinal Step 1, try to specifically "identify the problem."
Ask yourself: How do I feel? Left out of fun things? Trapped by daily responsibilities? Just plain lonely?

When does that feeling occur? At certain times? During certain events?

How do you relate to others that express similar feelings?

Record these thoughts. Spend some time thinking about them.

Make a list of things you would like to do that you are not doing.

Discuss your feelings with others:

    a.   A physician or counselor may be best to help sort out some of this and/or refer you for other help if needed.

b. If professional help is not available or if you believe not necessary, talk to friends and others that you can trust and feel comfortable talking with about it.

c. If there is no one you feel comfortable talking to, you have identified the problem.

d. If there are two of you, talk frankly with each other.

Now, write down the things you have identified that apply to you. If loneliness is on the list, it is something we can work on. Do not worry if you do not have anything earthshaking or extensive at this point. More will appear as we work our way along.

Cardinal Step 2 is to "assemble the facts." Important facts will probably have appeared in answering the questions addressed in identifying the problem. Nevertheless, ask yourself these questions:

a. What do I do every day—what is my routine?

b. Does my daily routine involve interaction with others?

c. Are my interactions with others heathy ones for me? Today, social media is a factor in any discussion of personal interactions. If one is not alert, one can gradually interact only with other people that are overwhelmed by their problems and need professional help. Getting out of that downward spiral may be needed. Step back and stay out of the fray for a few days. It may be amazing what new things will open!

d. Think about your gifts. How can they assist
    you in finding good interactions with people
    that you would like to be with, talk with and
    "hang out" with?
e. What do you enjoy? Are you doing those
    things?
f. What are your interests? Are you pursuing
    those that involve others?
g. What is realistic? What are some things you can
    realistically do to meet and interact with
    others?
h. Share your ideas and thoughts with others if
    you can and are comfortable.
i. Now dream a bit. What are you missing?
j. Finally, think about ways you can use your gifts
    to help others.

Write all your answers and thoughts down. Then, try
to write a paragraph that summarizes those thoughts
(facts) that apply to you and would help you climb out
of the lonely feelings of today. Limit it to positive
things that when acted upon will engage you in a
positive way with others. Can you condense this into
one sentence? The "one sentence" exercise is
worthwhile, but, if you cannot condense things that far,
that is fine.

The product of the exercise of condensing your
thoughts can serve as your guide for the next steps. If
you were unable to do the condensing as suggested, do
not stop there. The next Cardinal Steps will help sort
through everything.

Cardinal Step 3 is to analyze the facts you have identified related to the loneliness. This is more than just to think about them. It is time to apply the "Tools of Faith" in a planned and methodical way. The Bible is the place to start. Do some searches that include the words "Bible" and "lonely" or "loneliness." Pages and pages of citations and links will appear. Read some of these. I bet a few will capture your attention and thoughts. Do similar searches for key words that appear in your lists and especially those in your summary paragraph or sentence. Use the word "Bible" with some and not with others. Make sure you focus on positive things. Identify actions on your part that might engage you in a positive, interesting, fulfilling or fun way with others.

Loneliness is not just a product of modern times. It has been a problem for people forever. Scholars debate whether the writer of Ecclesiastes was King Solomon or another person or philosopher. We do not need to address that involved discussion here. No matter who the writer was, the messages confront everyday problems we all deal with today.

Ecclesiastes 4:7–10 provides tough but important guidance when dealing with the loneliness we are discussing:

> [7] Again, I saw vanity under the sun: [8] the case of solitary individuals, without sons or brothers; yet there is no end to all their toil, and their eyes are never satisfied with riches. [9] Two are better than one because they have a good reward for their toil. [10] For if they fall, one will

lift the other, but woe to one who is alone and falls and does not have another to help.

It is so true. All the riches in the world will not defeat loneliness. The value of a friend is far greater.

This does not solve the problem, but it does provide pointed focus. Personal relationships are very important. Developing those relationships and keeping them can make a real difference. Thoughtful study of material from your search on loneliness is the next step. It also means to take the time to expand your search and look for more articles by counselors, physicians and other trained specialists. Moreover, talking about your feelings with others will surprise you. Many people have had the same feelings.

Make notes as you progress and identify the thoughts, suggestions and points that make sense and seem to apply to you. Do not get in a hurry. It takes time for things to resolve. The idea that God works on God's time, not necessarily your time, is ever so true. Forcing a result usually does not work. It will happen, just let it have its own time.
Look over your notes. Where are they leading you?

Cardinal Step 4 is to "develop alternatives" for solving the loneliness "problem." First and foremost, engage in prayer. That may sound like an empty exercise. I suspect most of us have felt that way from time to time. But, it really does work. Give it serious effort. Spend the time to have a real talk in your mind with God. It will help.

The "get yourself right with…" exercise will also help. Who knows—"I" might be part of my problem. Truly loving yourself and being proud of yourself for who and what you are will pay dividends in many ways. None of us is perfect; the people that will make a difference in helping cure your loneliness are going to be willing to put the past behind. Ask yourself: Am I grumpy a lot? Do I blame others for many of my problems? These questions, and others you will ask as you read and pray, may lead to a realization that "getting right with yourself," then others and always with God is one key to curing loneliness. So, make sure your take yourself through that entire process.

Following all the steps through Cardinal Step 4 will yield a helpful result. A problem has been identified and focus of thought and time have been applied. The Bible and related relevant sources have been identified and studied. Prayer has been with us all the way. We have worked at "getting right" and cleaned house of old baggage. Alternatives have been identified. They have been listed and re-thought. You have considered yourself and made some changes in thinking. You are working at being one that others can interact with easily and in a spirit that lifts both of you up. Things are about to change.

You now have alternatives and ideas to step out into the world and try. The action item of this Cardinal Step 5 can be the hardest. Since Aristotle, at least, scientists and thinkers, including Newton, Galileo and Einstein, have recognized what is known as "inertia." The Cambridge Academia Content Dictionary defines it in physics as the force that causes something moving to tend to continue moving, and that causes something not moving to tend to continue not to move."

As with many scientific rules, they soon are applied to parallels in everyday life. That is true of the use of the term "inertia." That same Cambridge dictionary includes this definition as applied to life: "The tendency not to change what is happening."

Engineers know that a significant force is required to get an object that is stationary to start motion. My body tells me that every time I get up after sitting for a while! My mind also tells me how hard it is for me to change something I have done routinely for a long time. It is even harder to get me to step out and get moving on something I have not done before!

Nevertheless, Cardinal Step 5 involves overcoming inertia and relying on your gifts to try out the alternatives you have developed. Sitting back and looking at the list does not work. Keep in mind "out" can mean many different things and does not always require leaving your home. It means acting. A call, a text, a positive post—these all can be getting "out" and doing things with and for others. Whatever your situation, apply the force necessary to overcome the inertia AND:

"Go for it!" That is Cardinal Step 6. Pick the best alternatives—loneliness is not a part of those! The very act of trying alternatives can solve the loneliness problem. You will be interacting with others in a positive way. Loneliness will not last long!

Chapter X: "We can know God *truly*"

One of my assignments in a seminary course was to discuss the statement "We cannot know everything there is to know about God, but we can know God truly." I first looked to the Oxford dictionary for definitions of the word "truly." It is defined as: "truthful," "to the fullest degree" and "genuinely." After completing the assignment, and upon further reflection, I realized my thoughts, as they developed, sum up my progression to the thoughts I have shared in this book.

Much of what I know about God I "know" from reading the Bible and studying the understandings of those of faith. My own personal faith has matured to the point of asking the question:" What is "faith"?

Many have attempted to describe it. John Calvin defines faith in The Institutes, Book III as: "The firm statement and certain knowledge of God's benevolence toward us, founded upon the truth of the freely given promise in Christ, both revealed to our minds and sealed upon our hearts by the Holy Spirit."

It is hard to think of anything left out of that comprehensive description of faith. When looking for a simpler, easier to articulate description, I like Dr. Cynthia Rigby's description of Karl Barth's view, that "faith is a gift from God," a kind of "surplus grace."

Dr. Rigby is a professor at Austin Presbyterian Theological Seminary. She sums up faith in her own straightforward way after thoughtfully and eloquently discussing the views of Barth, Calvin and several others in her book *Holding Faith*: "It is faith that will never let us go because it is an overflow of the unconditional love of God. It is with the confidence that God's got us—even when we doubt or are skeptical—that we forge ahead."

Although there are books and books that try to go further, I think this is about all I need to understand what faith is about. My shorthand summary is that faith is the overriding comfort from knowing God that things are going to be okay—no matter what.

How would you describe "faith"?

Let us now "forge" ahead: How do we apply this to describing knowing God, "truly"? Dr. Rigby addresses this topic in observing, "Our theological language reflects the fact we know *something* true, but not *everything*, about the mystery that is God." That is a thought like where I stand on this discussion. I know something about it all and have the comfort that God loves me, but know I have a lot more to learn.

In fact, we humans all have more to learn. Think about Newton, who discovered much about basic earthbound physics. And Galileo, who discovered the true nature of earth's relationship to the Sun. Both were controversial at first, and later were considered revolutionary in our understanding of our world at the time. Then, along comes Albert Einstein, who puts a whole new perspective on our understanding of the universe. The Webb telescope's first pictures have provided new information on the early universe and raised even more questions about the universe. On the other end of the physical spectrum, quantum physics has opened up all sorts of as-yet-unanswered questions about the physical underpinnings of everything down to the smallest parts of matter.

I mention these things only to point out these are examples of how we, over time, learn more about the scientific nature of what God created. It stands to reason we can expect to learn more and more as we humans progress in our faith journey. I suspect our understandings of science and faith are related and are progressing somewhat together. For example, Galileo's understanding of the earth's relationship to the sun opened the door to our understanding we are not physically located at the center of everything. Nevertheless, we are just as important as ever as a part of the body of Christ. We are learning more and more about that and our responsibilities.

Calvin attempts to categorize our understanding when he uses the terms "general revelation" and "special revelation." In short, I look at this as meaning everyone can know there is a God (general revelation) but those that know God are those that God is further revealed to in Jesus Christ (special revelation). Some take this further and say that a special revelation means that Christ is revealed to only a few in a special way. I caution that those who believe they have a special revelation at times carry that to an extreme and are unable or unwilling to look at or hear those they view as on the outside. A feeling of infallibility can also appear. (I fear this may have contributed to the fall of many churches and church leaders in the past.) I try to spend my time focusing on what we are asked to do by our faith, for ourselves and all others than what "special" place it has made for me. I suggest the "special revelation" through Jesus Christ opens the door for each of us to play a role in making life "special" for all. Just as we learn something new nearly every day about our world, we will learn more and more about our role as a part of the body of Christ. As we read, listen, learn and live in a faith revealed to us through Christ, we will find that comfort we seek.

How is it that we can know God truly? It is clear to me it is like love. It is not something I can fully describe. In fact, that, for me, has been a kind of "revelation." If we live by doing, and doing while caring, and helping, and teaching, and learning, and sharing and loving, there is an indescribable comfort and "genuine" good feeling that arises from within. The fullness of our God-given life, a bit of heaven on earth, appears like grace, as a gift that is just there—sometimes when we least expect it. That, I believe, is how we can know God to the fullest degree possible—"to know God *truly*"! It is as simple as that. So, that is enough—for me at least!

I learned more than I would have ever guessed that cold winter morning. Take the time to notice and think about the unique moments of beauty that appear. Your "Cardinal in the Snow" may be just around the corner.

Resources

Brooks, Garth. "Unanswered Prayers." *No Fences*. Capitol Nashville. 1990, compact disc.

Calvin, John. *The Institutes, Book III*. Moscow, ID: Canon Press, 2020. First published 1559 by Reinolde Vvolf & Richarde Harisson (London).

Cambridge Dictionary. Cambridge Academic Content Dictionary. Cambridge University Press. https://dictionary.cambridge.org/dictionary/english/inertia.

Graham, Billy. "Prayer 101: How do I talk to God?" Billy Graham Evangelistic Association, 2021.

Hawking, Stephen W. *A Brief History of Time*. New York: Bantam Books, 1988.

Kushner, Harold S. *When Bad Things Happen To Good People*. New York: Schocken Books, 1981.

Lewis, C. S. *Letters to Malcolm: Chiefly on Prayer*. San Diego, CA: Harvest, 1964.

———. *Mere Christianity*. Rev. ed. New York: Simon & Schuster, 1952.

Merriam-Webster Dictionary. Last updated August 13, 2022.

https://www.merriam-webster.com/dictionary/righteous.

Oxford English Dictionary. 2nd ed. Oxford: Oxford University Press, 1989.

Rigby, Cynthia L. *Holding Faith.* Nashville, TN: Abingdon Press, 2018.

About the Author

John Kenney lives in Oklahoma City with his wife, Jane. They have two children and six grandchildren. John obtained degrees in engineering and law from the University of Oklahoma. In 2020, he received a Certificate In Ministry from Austin Presbyterian Theological Seminary, where he now serves on the Board of Directors.

John worked as a manufacturing engineer before attending law school. His law career has involved work on matters and cases in litigation involving engineering, science and technology. He has received numerous honors and awards related to his work as a lawyer and in his community.

John is the inventor of ten patents issued by the United States Patent Office. He is also a country music songwriter whose copyrighted works have been recorded by singer-songwriter and collaborator Bob Fraley for the debut album "Bootjack Romeo," and his own album, "My Top Advice." His Christian children's songs have been recorded by Parker and Alexander in their album "All of Us."

John currently serves as a Preaching Elder in Indian Nations Presbytery of the Presbyterian Church (U.S.A.). He is an Elder and past Deacon and Trustee of Westminster Presbyterian Church in Oklahoma City. He teaches and leads Sunday School and Bible study classes for groups in several churches and organizations. He also preaches at churches in the Indian Nations Presbytery.

Printed in the USA
CPSIA information can be obtained
at www.ICGtesting.com
LVHW011405041023
759662LV00001B/1

9 781960 326201